GOD
IN THE
DARK

GOD
IN THE
DARK

*The Assurance of Faith
Beyond A Shadow
of Doubt*

OS GUINNESS

CROSSWAY

WHEATON, ILLINOIS

God in the Dark

Published by Crossway
    1300 Crescent Street
    Wheaton, Illinois 60187

Cover illustration: Raymond Elliott

Cover design: Cindy Kiple

Art Direction: Mark Schramm

First printing, 1996

Printed in the United States of America

Scripture quotations are from The New English Bible. © The Delegates of the Oxford University Press and The Syndics of The Cambridge University Press 1961, 1970. Reprinted

Acknowledgment is made to the following for permission to reprint copyrighted material: From *Knots* by R. D. Laing, the poem "If I Don't Know . . . I Don't Know," copyright © 1970 by the R. D. Laing Trust; reprinted by permission of Tavistock Publications Limited and Pantheon Books, A Division of Random House, Inc. Four lines from "The Free Thinker" from *The Collected Poems of G. K. Chesterton*; reprinted by permission from Miss D. E. Collins and Dodd Mead and Co., Inc.

Library of Congress Cataloging-in-Publication Data
Guinness, Os
   God in the dark : the assurance of faith beyond a shadow of
doubt / Os Guiness.
      p.   cm.
   Includes bibliographical references and index.
   ISBN 13: 978-0-89107-845-6 (alk. paper)
   ISBN 10: 0-89107-845-2
   1. Faith. I. Title.
BT774.G85   1996
231'.042—dc20   95-41684

Crossway is a publishing ministry of Good News Publishers.
C H   21   20   19   18   17   16   15   14   13

D.O.M

and in memory of
my mother,
a woman of deep faith
who magnificently fulfilled
her motto,
"Live a life of love."

CONTENTS

———■|———

PART ONE

∎|

I AM, THEREFORE
I DOUBT

I BELIEVE
IN DOUBT

The simplest things in life are often the most profound. Sometimes I feel on fire with the immensity of this: Each of us is a person—alive, growing, and relating. From the moment we wake to the moment we fall asleep, we think, we feel, we choose, we speak, we act, not as isolated individuals but as persons among people.

And underneath everything lie dependency and trust. From a baby with its mother, to friendships of children, to neighbors in community, to agreements among nations, life depends on trust. Counting on people is trust. Enjoying people is trust. Trust is the shared silence, the exchanged look, the expressive touch. Crying for help is trust; shaking hands is trust; a kiss is trust. The highest reaches of love and life depend on trust. Are there any questions more important to each of us than, *Whom do I trust? How can I be sure?*

We can devise a thousand strategies—such as law—to help us flee from trust. We can summon up scores of reasons—

such as suspicion—to protect us from vulnerability to trust. But we have all once known the experience of complete dependence and complete trust—with our mothers at the beginning of life. And we can all know similar dependence and trust at the summit of our lives—in our free acknowledgment of God, when we receive his gift of faith as a trust that arises out of utter dependence on him.

All of which is why when trust goes and doubt comes in such a shadow is cast, such a wound is opened, such a hole is left, such anxiety gnaws.

God is not only a person, he is the supreme person on whom all personhood depends, not to speak of life itself and our entire existence. That is why to know him is to trust him, and to trust him is to begin to know ourselves. That is why our chief end is to glorify God and enjoy him forever. It is also why trusting God in the dark is so hard, and doubting God is so devastating. For when trust and dependence turn into doubt, it is as if the sun is eclipsed, the compass needle wavers without a north, and the very earth that was so solid moves as in an earthquake.

I have met some people who are on the road to faith who doubt God because they want to believe but dare not. How would you feel if someone flew more than halfway around the world to say to you, "I am at a loss. Life has no meaning unless God is there. There is hardly anyone left whom I can trust. Will you help me in my search?" I well remember a man on our doorstep in London who had crossed the world for this very reason. It was deeply sobering because I knew that after his previous failures to find answers he had cried out louder and more often, and the scars of the razor blades were still on his wrists to show it. What would you say? How would you help him? How would you introduce him to God who would never let him down, especially since God was less certain to him than human beings who had let him down?

I have met other people who are backing away from faith in God and doubt God because they do not want to believe but still do. I will never forget a woman who sat in our living room when we lived in Switzerland. She argued; she cried; she pounded the floor. Why should she trust God? He was a monster; a hard, unyielding monarch; a Mafia boss whose power was everywhere; a merciless creditor who demanded his pound of flesh. Hadn't she tried to obey? Hadn't she given it everything? But the more she saw God the more she feared, and the more she feared the more she became angry, and the angrier she became the more she hated, and the more she hated the more afraid of God she grew.

She knew she was caught in a vicious trap, sliding down a slippery spiral. She was young; she was loved; she was successful. But none of it made any difference. She could not trust God. She could not trust with real rest and without reservations. And in the bitterness of doubt, her spirit was like darkness at noon.

The doubts of these two people were entirely different, but they were both doubting God for the same reason: They did not know God as he really is. The man, however, knew that he did not know, while the woman thought that she did. Her picture of God (which came from experiences in the past) was so distorted that, without realizing it, she was believing a grotesque caricature of God that, for sanity's sake, she was forced at the same time to doubt.

Fortunately, she is not in that position today. She has come to know God as he is; she is able to trust him, and her whole life reflects the difference. In later chapters we will examine doubts like these in depth to see how they arise and how they can be resolved. They are only two types of doubt among many others, but they introduce us directly to the heart of our problem.

Doubt is not simply intellectual, an abstract philosophical or theological question. Nor is it merely psychological, a state of morbid spiritual or psychological anxiety. Doubt is personal. Doubt is all about people—who they are and what they say. At its most basic, doubt is a matter of truth, trust, and trustworthiness. Can we trust God? Are we sure? How can we be sure? Do we trust him enough to depend on him utterly? Are we trusting him enough to enjoy him? Is the whole of living different for that trust?

THE VALUE OF UNDERSTANDING DOUBT

Part of the glory of the Christian faith is that at its heart is a God who is a person. "He who is," the father of Jesus Christ and our father, is infinite, but he is also personal. The Christian faith therefore places a premium on the absolute truthfulness and trustworthiness of God, so understanding doubt is extremely important to a Christian. Of course, faith is much more than the absence of doubt, but to understand doubt is to have a key to a quiet heart and a quiet mind. Anyone who believes anything will automatically know something about doubt. But those who know why they believe are also in a position to discover why they doubt. The follower of Christ should be such a person. Not only do Christians believe, they are those who "think in believing and believe in thinking," as Augustine expressed it. The world of Christian faith is not a fairy-tale, make-believe world, question-free and problem-proof, but a world where doubt is never far from faith's shoulder.

Consequently, a healthy understanding of doubt should go hand in hand with a healthy understanding of faith. We ourselves are called in question if we have no answer to doubt. If we constantly doubt what we believe and always believe-yet-doubt, we will be in danger of undermining our personal integrity, if not our stability. But if ours is an examined faith, we should be unafraid to doubt. If doubt is eventually justified, we were believing what clearly was not worth believing. But if doubt is answered, our faith grows stronger still. It knows God more certainly, and it can enjoy God more deeply. Faith is not doubt-free, but there is a genuine assurance of faith that is truly beyond a shadow of doubt.

Obviously then, each one of us should understand doubt for God's sake and for ours. God is to be trusted, yet we human beings are prone to doubting: That is justification enough for trying to understand doubt. But an understanding of doubt will also bring two particular benefits to followers of Christ today.

First, a healthy understanding of doubt will act as a safeguard against today's widespread and unnecessary breakdown of faith. Christians are confronted by a situation that militates openly against assured faith. In most modern countries, public life has grown more secular and private life more pluralistic. In the Western part of the modern world, the Christian foundations of Western culture have been torn up and discarded. Our Christian past is in disrepute, and the very basis for any faith, Christian or otherwise, is held to be discredited in thinking circles. At the same time the vacuum created by collapsing Christendom has been filled by a bewildering variety of alternative faiths, facing us with a jostling and anxiety-creating pluralism. Many of us are also smarting emotionally under the sting of reactions to our faith and are keenly aware of the intellectual deficiency in our response.

In such a situation, it is hardly surprising if at times we falter as believers in a disbelieving age. This state of affairs has aggravated the already serious problem of doubt among Christians. Some, in response, have abandoned the faith altogether; many more have kept the faith but abandoned all pretense of any intellectual component. The loss of faith has not been stanched, and this has suggested that the Christian faith is a fragile, vulnerable belief with little intellectual integrity. This suggestion, in its turn, lends support to the common rejection of the Christian faith among thinking people. What is most damaging is not that Christians doubt but that there seems to be so little honesty about doubt and so little understanding of how to resolve it. This must be changed.

Second, a healthy understanding of doubt helps us to prepare for the years of testing that, I believe, are to come. Faith at its truest is radical reliance on God. It is a conviction born of understanding, grounded solidly in the truth of who God is and what he has said and done. But what our faith "should be" may be far removed from what our faith "is." In practice, many of us have become Christians and are continuing to believe for less than the best reasons and clearest motives. This will have serious consequences in the critical years ahead when the civilizational conflicts deepen and the battle between God and the gods grows more intense.

For example, one person's faith may be a genuine trust in God but also a trust in certain Christian friends, while another person has truly committed to God and also to the care of a strong local church or Christian community. Or again, others may honestly put themselves under the Lordship of Christ, yet at the same time adhere passionately to some aspect of the Christian way of life that by temperament or nationality they would be likely to espouse anyway.

In each specific case it is impossible to determine the exact line of distinction between faith and faith plus, between our faith in God and our faith in other people and things. Where faith is not as strong or as pure as it should be, it is not illegitimate. If our motives had to be spring-water pure, which of us would pass the test? But impure faith that is weak or wrongly based is always vulnerable in a crisis. To the degree that other motives are also at work, faith is not radical reliance on God alone. Seen in this light, every test that shows us what we are really relying on can be constructive. If testing shows that our attachment to

Christian friends or to a particular lifestyle or culture is stronger than our attachment to God himself, we must ask whether these supports for faith are in danger of becoming substitutes. What we need, then, is to be stopped short before the process of substitution is complete and faith becomes altogether empty.

THE SQUARE ONE PRINCIPLE

Jesus challenged the Jews of his day with a searching question: "How can you have faith so long as you receive honor from one another, and care nothing for the honor that comes from him who alone is God?"[1] Ostensibly their faith was solely in God, but that faith was only nominal. In reality, their faith was in each other. More precisely, their nominal faith in God was supported and accredited by a closed system of mutual human honoring that made the need for any honor from God superfluous.

We should ask similar questions of ourselves, particularly those of us who are Western Christians. What sort of faith do we have? How can we know how strong our faith really is so long as we are comparatively untroubled in a world of material affluence, social ease, and spiritual privilege? Or to reverse it, could it be that in the deepening turbulence of our generation God is not only judging a culture that has abandoned him but also, as it were, shaking up the bag and testing the foundations to see if we Christians are as ready as we think for the critical years ahead?

The coin has two sides. Much of the weakening and breakdown of faith we are witnessing is a logical consequence, pure and simple, of the deep deficiency of faith today. On the other hand, it may also be a sign of God's hidden sovereignty and wisdom preparing us for a tougher future.

Long-standing supports are crumbling, and many of the accepted assumptions of normal Western life are being shaken—such as social stability and a reasonable prosperity.

We are forced to see the true foundations of our faith (that is, our practical rather than professed faith, our day-to-day trust, our matter-of-fact belief, our down-to-earth reliance). Far better to be tested today and have the chance to put right what is shown to be wrong than to be tested tomorrow and be found wanting.

The issues we are facing in the present crisis of faith touch on what I call the *Square One Principle*. Life can proceed with deceptive ease on the basis of a faith that was once vital but has become so taken for granted that it is no longer authentic. At that stage any pressure may be such a test for faith that the believer is faced with a choice: Give up or go back to square one. If we give up, then we abandon faith altogether. But if we go back to square one (and so back to our roots, back to our foundations, back to our beginning), we will find a faith that is solid and secure. The lesson of the Square One Principle is this: The person who has the courage to go back when necessary is the one who goes on in the end.

Richard Sibbes, the Puritan writer, put it this way: "Christ's work, both in the church and in the hearts of Christians, often goeth backward that it may go the better forward. As seed roots in the ground in the winter time, but after comes better up, and the harder the winter the more flourishing the spring, so we learn to stand by falls, and get strength by weakness discovered—*virtutis custos infirmitas*—we take deeper root by shaking."[2]

Seen this way, the collapse of Christendom is a blessing for the Christian faith, and the present crisis of faith may be the best opportunity for the gospel in centuries, at least for Christians in the West. But to use this opportunity fully we must stop the severe hemorrhaging of faith among believers; we must provide decisive answers to the questions and objections of our contemporaries; and we must work toward a clearly discernible Christian response to the crises of civilization. Developing a fresh understanding of the old problem of doubt is a key contribution to this.

GOAL AND APPROACH

What is faith? What is an assured, understanding faith that is strong, true, and beyond a shadow of doubt? And what is the misunderstanding or mistreatment of faith that causes doubt, and how can it be avoided? And, above all, what does it mean to let faith be faith to such an extent that it will, in turn, let God be God? These are the questions we will examine, and that is our goal—to let God be God.

What will be our approach in this book? In Part One (the first two chapters) we will examine the nature of doubt, setting it off clearly from common misconceptions that cloud the issue today.

Part Two (Chapters 3 to 9) is the heart of our discussion. Here we will examine the seven most common categories of doubt and develop a framework in which we can understand and analyze all our specific doubts.

In Part Three (the last two chapters) we will look at two doubts that are probably the supreme doubts of all believers in all times: the doubts that come from two torturous questions, "Why, O Lord?" and "How long, O Lord?"

Getting to the heart of doubt is rather like peeling a chestnut: It's worthwhile in the end, but it entails getting through a prickly layer. The prickles surrounding doubt are the layers of misunderstanding that obscure what doubt is—and one misunderstanding above all: the common idea that doubt is wrong and we should feel guilty about doubting because doubt is another word for unbelief.

Once we have torn away these layers of misunderstanding we can get to the kernel of doubt and see not only its dangers but its value. Then, since we find there is no believ-ing without some doubting and since believing is all the stronger for understanding and resolving doubt, we can say as Christians that if we doubt in believing it is also true that we believe in doubting. René Descartes got things exactly the wrong way round. The truth is not that "I doubt, therefore I am" but "I am, therefore I doubt."

————■————

CHAPTER 2

DARE
TO DOUBT

Once when I was traveling in Southern Europe I witnessed the proverbial sight of a peasant beating his donkey. The peasant was walking behind, driving his donkey on. Huge bales of firewood were strapped to its back, but the donkey forced its way up the steep little path that served as a village street. Gradually the animal slowed, exhausted. Spurred on again by a stream of oaths, it staggered a few paces further and sank to the ground, defeated, and lay there panting in the relentless sun. It was then that the peasant beat it—and beat it and beat it and beat it again.

Many Christians treat faith like that. Believe this! Believe that! Stop doubting and believe more firmly! Admonitions and warnings are piled onto faith's back until it can take no more. Cajolings then give way to threats and threats to the big stick until, undernourished and overloaded, their faith sinks to the ground and expires.

We might ask which is worse: the cruelty or the stupidity? Which sadder: the plight of faith and the donkey or the plight of the owner? But this is not a book about donkeys or even about faith—at least not directly. It is a book about doubt. Yet what is doubt but faith suffering from mistreatment or malnutrition? Concern for the prevention of doubt is automatically concern for the prevention of cruelty to faith. The way to get the best out of something—whether faith or a donkey or anything else—is to find out what it is and treat it accordingly. Mistake it for something else or push it beyond its limits and its purpose may be destroyed. Ask it to do more than it can and it may not do what it should. Donkeys have no objection to donkey work, but they cannot stand to be taken for racehorses or tractors.

As soon as we ask what faith is and what sort of mistreatment of faith causes doubt, we are led to the first major misconception about doubt—the idea that doubt is always wrong because it is the opposite of faith and the same thing as unbelief. What this error leads to is a view of faith that is unrealistic and a view of doubt that is unfair.

Doubt is then the jackass of the world of faith. Like the donkey, it is despised by its enemies and mistreated by its friends, but only because it is bound to be treated unfairly when it is seen unrealistically. The injustice is that the donkey is beaten until it collapses and then it is beaten *for collapsing.* In the same way many Christians drive their faith unfairly when they believe, and then they flog their faith unmercifully when they doubt. In both cases they do this because they have been led to believe that true faith is doubt-free and that doubt is the same thing (and just as sinful) as unbelief.

In short, we must remind ourselves of a simple, opening truth when we doubt, especially those of us who are more conscientious or more conservative. Many Christians have specific doubts, but that is not the deepest problem. Over and above specific doubts, they feel guilty and ashamed at having doubts at all and that is what torments their faith. They do not understand what doubt is. And that, however dangerous doubt may be, it is not something to be ashamed of.

THE HEART OF DOUBT IS A DIVIDED HEART

What is doubt? And how is it related to faith and unbelief? Our English word *doubt* comes from the Latin *dubitare*, which is rooted in an Aryan word meaning "two." So we can start by defining our terms like this: To believe is to be "in one mind" about trusting someone or something as true; to disbelieve is to be "in one mind" about rejecting them. To doubt is to waver between the two, to believe and disbelieve at once and so to be "in two minds."

This two-ness or double-ness is the heart of doubt and the deepest dilemma it represents. *The heart of doubt is a divided heart.* This is not just a metaphor. It is the essence of the Christian view of doubt, and human language and experience from all around the world also bear it out.

In English the double-ness of doubt is pictured in phrases such as "having a foot in both camps." There are many equivalents in other languages. The Chinese picture of irresolution is humorous as well as graphic. They speak of a person "having a foot in two boats." In the Peruvian Andes the Huanuco Quechuas speak of "having two thoughts" and the Shipibos further to the east have an expression, "thinking two things." In Guatemala the Kekchi language describes the doubter as a man "whose heart is made two," while the Navajo Indians in the Southwestern United States use a similar term, "that which is two with him."[1]

The Greek words in the New Testament that are translated into English as "doubt" are equally fascinating. Examining root meanings is not everybody's cup of tea, but it is worthwhile here because it sheds so much light on the nature of doubt. Notice that in each case there is an unmistakable emphasis on the ambivalence or double-mindedness of doubt.

One word *(dipsukos)* speaks of a person who is chronically double minded. James describes such a doubter as "a heaving sea ruffled by the wind"[2] A second word *(diakrino)* is the stronger form of the word to *sunder* or to *separate*. This word can convey several meanings, but one of them expresses an inner state of mind so torn between various options that a person cannot make up his or her mind. Jesus uses this word when he says to his disciples, "Have faith in God. I tell you this: if anyone says to this mountain, 'Be lifted from your place and hurled into the sea,' and has no *inward doubts*, but believes that what he says is happening, it will be done for him"[3]

A third word *(meteorizomai)* means "to raise" or "to suspend," when it is used literally (as it is in the root of our modern word meteor). Or it can mean "to raise a person's hopes" when it is used figuratively. But when it is used figuratively, it can also mean to soar or to lift oneself up, and so to be arrogant in spirit. And then, because one is lifted up in the air, it comes to mean to be unsettled and, therefore, restless, anxious, tense, and doubtful.

The last use of the word covers doubt. It describes a state of mind that is the result of an awkward position. Many modern expressions capture this ambivalence, such as being "up in the air" or being "hung up." When Jesus says to his disciples, "You are not to set your mind on food and drink; you are not to worry,"[4] he is saying that God's care for us as Father means that food and drink are not to be a hang-up, an occasion for doubt and anxiety that constantly keeps us up in the air.

A fourth word *(dialogizomai)* is the root of our word *dialogue*. Its own root is "thought," and from that it has come to mean the inner debate of a person who is reasoning with himself or herself. The word is usually used in the New Testament for internal reasoning that is wrong or evil. Jesus uses it when he confronts the disciples after his resurrection: "Why are you so perturbed?" he asks. "Why do *questionings* arise in your minds?"[5] The word opens a window into the debate raging in the councils of the disciples' hearts as they doubted. So long as there is doubt, the debate continues and the arguments fly back and forth. Only when the votes are cast is it clear whether faith's motion has been passed or defeated.

A fifth word *(distazo)* means doubt in the sense of hanging back, hesitating, or faltering. It expresses what we mean when we say that we have our reservations or vacillate about something. Matthew uses this word when he records that "Jesus at once reached out and caught hold of him, and said, 'Why did you *hesitate*? How little faith you have!'"[6] The same word is used of those who doubted the risen Christ: "When they saw him, they fell prostrate before him, though some were *doubtful*."[7] Genuine faith is unreserved in its commitment; doubt has reservations. Faith steps forward; doubt hangs back. Doubt holds itself open to all possibilities but is reluctant to close on any.

The combined force of all these phrases and words is inescapable. If people are "torn" between options, unable to "make up" their minds, or if they are "up in the air" over something and unsure which side they should "come down on," or if they are furiously "debating" with themselves or "hanging back," or weighing up their "reservations," they are nothing if not "in two minds." This condition of doubleness is the essence of doubt.

DOUBT IS NOT UNBELIEF

What follows from this observation is decisive for our whole discussion: Doubt is not the opposite of faith, nor is it the same as unbelief. Doubt is a state of mind in suspension *between* faith and unbelief so that it is neither of them wholly and it is each only partly. This distinction is absolutely vital because it uncovers and deals with the first major misconception of doubt—the idea that we should be ashamed of doubting because doubt is a betrayal of faith and a surrender to unbelief. No misunderstanding causes more anxiety and brings such bondage to sensitive people in doubt.

The difference between doubt and unbelief is crucial. The Bible makes a definite distinction between them, though the distinction is not hard and fast. The word *unbelief* is usually used of a willful refusal to believe or of a deliberate decision to disobey. So, while doubt is a state of suspension between faith and unbelief, unbelief is a state of mind that is closed against God, an attitude of heart that disobeys God as much as it disbelieves the truth. Unbelief is the consequence of a settled choice. Since it is a deliberate response to God's truth, unbelief is definitely held to be responsible. There are times when the word *unbelief* is used in Scripture to describe the doubts of those who are definitely believers but only when they are at a stage of doubting that is rationally inexcusable and well on the way to becoming full-grown unbelief.[8] Thus the ambiguity in the biblical use of unbelief is a sign of psychological astuteness and not of theological confusion.

So it is definitely possible to distinguish in theory between faith, doubt, and unbelief (to believe is to be in one mind, to disbelieve is to be in another, and to doubt is to be in two minds). But in practice the distinction is not always so clear-cut, especially when doubt moves in the direction of unbelief and passes over that blurred transition between the open-ended uncertainty of doubt and the close-minded certainty of unbelief.

But the overall thrust of the biblical teaching on doubt is plain. A variety of words are used but the essential point is the same. Doubt is a halfway stage. To be in doubt is to be in two minds, to be caught between two worlds, to be suspended between a desire to affirm and a desire to negate. So the idea of "total" or "complete" doubt is a contradiction in terms; doubt that is total is no longer doubt, it is unbelief.

Of course, we may call our doubt "total doubt" or charge it with being unbelief. But only if our purpose is to stop doubt short and see that it does not become unbelief. When the father of the demoniac boy cried out to Jesus, "I believe; help my unbelief!" he was condemning his own doubt as unbelief.[9] But his words have become a doubter's prayer for good reason. Jesus, who never responded to real unbelief, showed by answering his prayer and healing his son that he recognized it as doubt. The distinction between doubt and unbelief, though not hard and fast, is valid and useful. Its importance, however, is not that we know *when* doubt becomes unbelief. Only God knows that, and human attempts to say so can be cruel. But it means that we should be clear about *where* doubt leads to as it grows into unbelief.

SOFT OR HARD ON DOUBT

The heart of the Christian view of doubt is a healthy combination of an analysis of the nature of doubt and an awareness of where it leads. The former is encouraging and the latter sobering. But curiously, this combination is also the reason why people tend to be either "soft" on doubt or "hard" on doubt, and both can find biblical support for their views. The former can point to the great difference between doubt and unbelief and the latter to the great similarity. Each ignores the balancing emphasis of biblical teaching.

This balance sets apart the New Testament view from its Greek and Roman surroundings. The world of the first century was marked by a deep awareness of doubt, but usually it traced doubt back only to philosophical skepticism or cultural irreso-lution. In the New Testament, however, faith is synonymous with the obedience of faith, so that faith also involves both the understanding and the will. Doubt is therefore tackled primarily at the point of action and not solely at the point of reflection. It is just as much a matter of what we do as of what we know and how we know that we know.

The Old Testament laid special stress against disobey-ing—rather than doubting—God. But the New Testament is strongly against doubt itself and stronger still against unbelief. Now that God has revealed himself so fully in Christ, the value of the stakes of salvation are higher, and there is less excuse for lack of faith.

This combined emphasis—that doubt is not the same as unbelief but can lead naturally to it—allows us a mature han-dling of doubt that avoids the extremes of being too hard or too soft on doubt. Those who forget the first point fall into the error of being too hard. In equating doubt and unbelief, they make doubt the opposite of faith in a way that is true neither to the Bible nor to what we know of human knowledge. By insisting that only doubt-free faith can be counted as genuine faith, they misunderstand what knowledge and faith are. The perfection-ism in the demand is more destructive of genuine faith than the worst of doubts could ever be.

The true relationship of faith and doubt is closer to that of courage and fear. Fear is not the opposite of courage, cowardice is. Fear, in fact, need be no final threat to courage. What courage cannot afford is recklessness. Take a mountain climber, a Grand Prix racing driver, or a person conquering a devastating disabil-ity. Each one has a courage that controls his or her fear and sub-dues his or her emotions so that risks are made responsible and commitments in the face of danger are carefully calculated.

It is the same with faith and doubt. Doubt is not the opposite of faith, unbelief is. Doubt does not necessarily or automatically mean the end of faith, for doubt is *faith in two minds*. What destroys faith is the disobedience that hardens into unbelief.

This is the second point that balances the first and safeguards it from the other extreme—being too soft on doubt. Doubt is not always fatal but it is always serious. Some people react so strongly against the morbid view of doubt that they treat doubt casually, even celebrate it. The error here is to isolate doubt from faith and unbelief and consider it strictly by itself as a mere mechanism of human knowing. The only question then asked is, *how* does doubt work? And the answer, since it is only abstract, carries little sting.

But the question is not abstract in real life, so to the interesting questions of *how* must be added the urgent question of *what*. As soon as this second question is asked (whom or what is being doubted?), the price of doubt rises or falls immediately. It is *whom* or *what* we doubt and not *how* we doubt that sets the market value of doubting.

If the object of our faith were as elusive as the Loch Ness monster or as inconsequential as whether to have a third cup of tea, then doubt makes little difference. But since the object of Christian faith is God, to believe or disbelieve is everything—at some points literally a matter of life and death. Thus the market value of doubt for the Christian is extremely high. Find out how seriously a believer takes his or her doubts and you have the index of how seriously he or she takes faith. For the Christian, doubt is not the same as unbelief, but neither is it divorced from it. Continued doubt loosens the believer's hold on the resources and privileges of faith and can be the prelude to the disasters of unbelief. So doubt is never treated as trivial.

DOUBTING IS AS DOUBTING DOES

What follows in Part Two is not meant to be a gloomy cataloging of specific doubts but a look at seven of the most common "families" of doubt. These "seven deadly doubts" are not an exhaustive account of doubt. Such a task would be herculean and quixotic. They are a broad overview of the main types of doubt that Christians commonly face. These broad categories give us an overall perspective from which to view, handle, and resolve our specific doubts. It is then wise for each of us to become aware of the doubts to which we are most prone and carefully think through the issues involved in each case.

But before we look at the seven deadly doubts, three reminders are helpful. First, there is an inescapable personal dimension to doubt that categorizing doubt must never obscure. In other words, doubting is as doubting does—a doubt is as big and bad as it is to a person doubting.

The doubts are a kind of problem. And a curious thing about problems is that a problem is only a problem if it is a problem to someone. Problems strike us all differently. What is trivial to one person may raise titanic questions for someone else. Some people face doubt only if they find no answer; others trigger doubts merely by raising questions. What puzzles a philosopher and taxes his or her mind to distraction may look completely irrelevant or quite obvious to a business person or teacher—and vice versa. The point is not to judge who is right, but to meet and resolve whatever doubt is a problem to us at any moment.

IN SICKNESS AND HEALTH

Second, there are useful parallels between doubt and physical sickness. When people speak of doubt, medical images will pop up sooner or later as doubt is seen as a form of sickness of faith. This analogy can be helpful if it gives a visual dimension to our thinking. But if it is pressed too far, medical imagery can lead to a sense of inevitability and passiveness that is inappropriate in resolving doubt. The image, of course, centers on the fact that faith and doubt have something of the same curious relationship as health and sickness.

For a start, health is the opposite of death just as faith is of unbelief. Both faith and health turn on the importance of wholeness, and both are much less obvious than one might imagine. It is customary, for example, to enjoy them most when one is aware of them least. Since aspects of each can be understood better in the light of their absence, each may be noticed more when it is not there than when it is. In telling us what health and faith are *not*, sickness and doubt also tell us something of what health and faith should be.

Again, doubts are like sicknesses in that the prevalent types vary from country to country, season to season, and climate to climate. Every believer is prone to doubt, but some are more prone to one kind and some to another. This should not leave us dispirited. We all get sick, but we do not live in fear of catching every known disease. Life would be miserable if we did. Still, if we travel in an infected area we would be foolish not to take precautions.

In the same way, assurance of faith depends on our grasp of God and his faithfulness and not on a mastery of all the doubts that are ever likely to assail us. Otherwise, faith could never be assured while one last doubt remained. But the alert believer should be aware of the main tendencies to doubt prevalent at the time. These will differ from generation to generation and from temperament to temperament, but it is wise to know the types of doubt to which we are most prone.

Or again, faith, like health, is best maintained by growth,

nourishment, and exercise and *not* by fighting sickness. Sickness may be the absence of health, but health is more than the absence of sickness, so prevention is better than cure. Leading a healthy life is more than being vaccinated for every possible disease. Equally, faith grows and flourishes when it is well-nourished and exercised, so the best way to resist doubt is to build up faith rather than simply to fight against doubt.

Lastly, there is as much danger in being preoccupied with doubt as with sickness. Preoccupation with sickness is not for those outside the medical profession. Otherwise, the preoccupation will become a sickness. Similarly, there is a real danger in fostering the doubter's equivalent of hypochondria. So even a book on doubt must not be read like a medical dictionary, or before long we may gloomily conclude that we are suffering from every doubt in the book.

GOD, NOT GOD-WORDS

Third, in resolving doubt we need to remember the difference between God and God-words. On one hand we can affirm without any reservations that *God is the answer to all doubt.* As Martin Luther said, in what must be the theological understatement of all time, "The Holy Spirit is not a sceptic."[10] Through the creative agency of his Word and his Spirit, God is the author and giver of faith; naturally he is the prime resolver of doubt. Faith is a gracious gift of God, and the resolution of doubt is a gracious gift of God.

This means that assurance of faith comes directly from knowing God and only indirectly from understanding doubt. (This is one reason why remarkably few books are written on doubt itself.) Understanding doubt is only a means to serve the end of true assurance of faith. More particularly, assurance of faith comes from knowledge of God, as objectively revealed in his Word and subjectively revealed by his Spirit. Who is it who gives us knowledge of our adoption into God's family? Who is it who is God's seal of faith in our hearts? Who is God's down payment on the inheritance we will receive in the future? Who is the first fruit of a harvest of blessings to come? The answer in each case is the Holy Spirit.[11] Without any hesitation, we can say that God is the answer to all doubt and that the largest part of doubting comes simply from not knowing or experiencing what God has said and done.

On the other hand, we can be too spiritual for our own good and confuse God with God-words. God is the answer to all doubt, but theologically correct God-answers are not necessarily the answer. Many people make a crucial mistake here. By exaggerating the theological dimensions of doubt, they obscure the spiritual, moral, psychological, and philosophical dimensions that are equally important.

It is an undeniable fact of Christian history that many believers have subscribed to a strong theology of assurance but have known no assurance themselves. Dr. Samuel Johnson, for example, suffered from such constitutional anxiety about his spiritual state that James Boswell said of him, he "saw God in clouds."[12] An even more poignant example is John Newton's close friend, William Cowper, the eighteenth-century poet and hymn writer who had a profound Calvinist theology but suffered from chronic suicidal depression. Are we to say that God's assurance is no more assured than the fluctuations of our feelings? Of course not. Or are we to insist that assurance of faith exists in a believer even when he or she is sure that such assurance does not exist? To some people this suggestion is paradoxical; to others it is nonsense. But much of the problem dissolves immediately once we recognize that there is a confusion of categories at its root. Some doubts are directly a matter of theology, others only indirectly, if at all.

This is a book on doubt and doubting; it is not a theology of assurance. The two are not the same. In fact, there are two types of people who in their doubt are particularly allergic to theological talk. On the one hand are those who are *insensitive* to God's truth. Their doubt is hardening into unbelief; merely to talk of God is to waste words, to pour water on a duck's back and watch it run off. Certainly they need conviction too but conviction of a different kind. On the other hand are those who are *over-sensitive*. They fasten on theological truths as on an armory of big sticks, and they rain down blows on their long-suffering faith, belaboring it for being substandard and for failing to believe what it should.

Theological answers, even though correct, can be unhelpful to both of these types of people, though for different reasons. Theological talk is only a verbal formula. Like a doctor's prescription, it needs to be taken to be a cure; like a recipe, it needs to be cooked to be eaten; like a check, it needs to be cashed to be spent. To the insensitive, theological talk seems as redundant as a prescription to a man who thinks he is well or a recipe to a man who is overfed or another check to a billionaire. To the over-sensitive, though, what matters is the cure, the meal, and the money.

This is why dispensing theological prescriptions is not the same thing as answering doubt. Our examination of doubt will always tell us two things: the deficiency of faith that has caused the problem, and the sufficiency of God that is needed as the answer. But the two need to be carefully related. God's grace can be as much misused when it is wrongly applied to those who are over-sensitive as when it is completely forgotten by those who are insensitive.

Let me stress that all the doubts we will discuss spring either from my own experience or from the experience of many who have shared their doubts with me. Over the last few decades I have talked with many hundreds who were suffering the deep anxieties of doubt. These doubts are not examined for academic purposes, nor are they treated in a critical way. Our aim here is to understand doubt in order to understand and to encourage faith. We do it in the same spirit in which John Bunyan's Christian and Hopeful erected a sign to keep other pilgrims from the hands of Giant Despair.

> *Over this stile is the way to Doubting Castle, which is kept by Giant Despair, who despiseth the King of the Celestial Country, and seeks to destroy his holy pilgrims.* Many therefore that followed after, read what was written, and escaped the danger.[13]

PART TWO

SEVEN FAMILIES
OF DOUBT

———■|———

CHAPTER 3

FORGETTING TO REMEMBER

Doubt from Ingratitude

Start a job badly and it immediately is that much harder to finish it well. Whether it's making a bed, building a skyscraper, or landing an astronaut on the moon, the lesson is the same. Leave some initial step undone, and it will be a handicap—or at least a factor—later in eventual failure. The same is true of Christian faith.

Many people doubt because they have left out something important in the way they have come to believe. Believe in God for wrong reasons or for no reason at all and you cannot expect to be free from doubt. The seven families of doubt illustrate this well. The first four are the direct result of deficiencies of faith in coming to believe and the last three are the result of deficiencies of faith in continuing to believe.

The heart has its reasons, Pascal wrote famously, of which reason knows nothing. This means that there is always more to knowing than human knowing will ever know. Which should make us wary of superficial descriptions of knowledge and faith. But there are at least four levels of understanding clearly discernible in a biblical view of faith and each of the first four categories of doubt runs parallel to one of these levels.

I am not saying that everyone who comes to faith in Christ does so by consciously thinking through these four levels. But consciously or unconsciously, the four levels must be built into any healthy faith. Notice that I am deliberately speaking of "levels of understanding" in believing, rather than "stages in believing." The stress is not only on the idea of progression (from lower to higher) but also on unbroken continuity. Basic to the idea of a level is the implication that a higher level goes beyond a lower level by including it, gathering it up, and building on it.

Just so, there are certain levels of understanding in coming to believe that the Christian faith is true, and these may bear no relation to the "stages" by which we have come to faith. But a healthy faith should include them all, and it should have each of them in its proper place. To confuse the order of these levels or to omit one or more of them is dangerous—not because our faith is then invalid, but because it does not rest on the strongest available foundations.

THE ONCE AND MIGHT HAVE BEEN

The first level of understanding necessary to faith is becoming critically aware of our dilemma in life without God. This sense of dilemma creates and constitutes a searcher. And for the searcher who goes on and comes to believe, this is the only possible starting point—a sense of need that may range from a mild discomfort to a deep conviction but that spurs someone to look for a solution beyond himself or herself.

Think back to your own conversion and how you began

to search for God, however vaguely. Until that point, did you take the gospel seriously as "good news"? Probably not. The reason was that you had little awareness of what a bad situation you were in. At least that was the case with me. Only when I began to realize what my situation was really like did I see the gospel for what it was—extremely good news for people in extremely bad situations. I don't know about you, but for me that discovery was an overwhelming experience that brought tears. This doesn't mean that we Christians *believe* in God because of our needs. What we do is *dis*believe in our previous worldview because of needs that our previous worldview can no longer answer. This is part of what makes our eventual faith in God (which we reach for other reasons) a radical reliance on God alone. Other points of reliance are ruled out from the start.

The Christian faith begins where all other faiths leave off. "How blest are those who know their need of God," Jesus exclaims, and as he opened the door to the kingdom of heaven, his listeners must have gasped.[1] The lintel is so low that the only people who can enter are those who are down on their knees. The prodigal son becomes the pattern for us all; he became so hungry that he was prepared to swallow his own pride. Yet that was the point at which he took his first step toward home. As Søren Kierkegaard noted simply, "God creates everything out of nothing—and everything which God is to use he first reduces to nothing."[2]

Without this first step there is no beginning, and every subsequent step in the search takes one further but in the same direction. So when the searcher eventually believes and becomes a Christian (I am ignoring for the moment the other levels of understanding that are involved), he or she is a person with a memory and a person of special gratitude. Whatever we may become, wherever we go, whatever we do, we should always be aware of what once was, what might have been, and what could well be again. For those of us who understand this, "By God's grace I am what I am" is never pious rhetoric.[3] "There but for the grace of God go I" is as realistic a statement as any we ever make.

This awareness of need is the first level of understanding in coming to faith, and if there is any deficiency at this level, a distinctive type of doubt will strike later on. What happens is that we begin well as Christians as we remember our past clearly. But then time passes, the memory fades and opportunities to doubt begin to come. As we fail to remember our previous situation, a slow and subtle change of heart takes place. What emerges is an attitude of resourcefulness that eventually grows into a mood of self-sufficiency and then into independence.

The effect is that what God has done fades slowly out of the picture, and we focus increasingly on what we ourselves seem able to do. That is, we continue to work with God, or maybe even without him, but the thought of self-sufficiency is not expressed so boldly. Finally, we reach a stage at which, whatever our external life is saying, our internal attitude is one of complete self-sufficiency.

THE PRESS RELEASE OF INGRATITUDE

At that point there is no need of a major crisis or a profound tragedy to precipitate doubt. All it takes is a little push, some minor inconvenience, a trifling price to pay for faith, some obligation or embarrassment involved in being a Christian, and suddenly a trail of doubts bubbles to the surface: "Maybe after all . . . ," "Perhaps I took it all a little too seriously. . . . Surely God can hardly expect me to. . . . ," "Probably I was a little overwrought, but I've weathered the crisis now. . . ."

Such doubts vary in intensity but bear united witness to a complacence or a disgruntled grumbling at any need for God and for his handling of our affairs.

The magic word that justifies these doubts is "phase" or "period," as if a stage has been reached where God is no longer necessary. But the key motif is ingratitude, a moral, spiritual, and emotional carelessness about what we once were and would be now apart from God. We become insensitive to what we might call the "once and might have been" of faith.

This was the chosen approach of the Evil One in tempting Eve, which should give us a healthy respect for its subtlety and danger. "Did God say . . . ?" he asked.[4] His innocent-sounding questions about the facts of the case were designed to open up the deeper issue of God's goodness. Why did God say this? Could it possibly be that his knowledge is power over you? Is God really as good as you have trusted him to be? Are you really as free as you would wish? Are you sure?

The questions bore in on Eve and shed a different light on her view of life, the first shadows on the familiar sunlit world of trust. Slowly the picture changes, and doubt is conceived at the first moment when "thank you" is superfluous. This is always the way: The oldest temptation is also the most contemporary. Writing in his *Notes from Underground* Dostoyevsky says of man, "If he is not stupid, he is monstrously ungrateful! Phenomenally ungrateful. In fact, I believe that the best definition of man is the ungrateful biped."[5]

Notice that this doubt is not purely spiritual, nor purely intellectual, nor purely emotional, but a little bit of all of them causing complete change of heart. The transformation is made up of spiritual, intellectual, and emotional elements that grow into an autonomous state of mind. Sooner or later this autonomy expresses itself in doubt. It has to in order to evade God's challenge to its existence. If I am to be autonomous, God must go.

The Apostle Paul described the autonomy of unbelief bluntly: "Knowing God, they have refused to honor him as God, or to render him thanks."[6] His words are a reminder that rebellion against God does not begin with the clenched fist of atheism but with the self-satisfied heart of the one for whom "thank you" is redundant. The bankruptcy of our position without God is forgotten, the sting of our former dilemma fades, a sense of God's conviction wears off, and our acknowledgment of God's grace becomes routine and matter-of-fact. But this process may be well underway before it becomes apparent. In fact, sometimes it is only when doubts are expressed openly that we have the first clue that things are no longer the same.

Doubts of this kind can be expressed in many ways, but they are usually notable for one feature—lack of urgency. There is no pain of loss in this doubt, no agonizing uncertainty, no straining desire for a solution. The desired goal is not recovery of faith but a respectable cover for retreat from faith. If people show deep concern that they are doubting in this way, it is a sign that they are not. This doubt is one of unconcern. It is insensitive, not over-sensitive.

Have you ever heard a husband on the verge of divorce finding fault with his wife, picking a quarrel, or blackening her name to others? What he is doing is laying the groundwork for the decisive moment and preparing his getaway. Hate, like love, picks up every shred of evidence to justify itself. Listen to the doubts of ingratitude in its terminal stage. They are not what they pretend to be. They are a backhanded note of dismissal, an explanation that is really an excuse. But not forever. At a certain point, there is no need for an alias or disguise. The ingratitude comes out into the open and sets as hard as marble. Not only is "thank you" superfluous, God is dismissed altogether.

A COMPUTER WOULD DO BETTER

Failure to remember is much more serious, of course, than a simple lapse of memory. The human mind is more than a computer. Computers have prodigious but dull and exact memories—what went in can come out again, exactly as it went in. But the human mind selects as well as stores. It not only receives, it picks and chooses and processes all it receives. So its own spiritual, moral, and psychological condition affects what it remembers.

Forgetfulness proves deadly because it strikes deep into the delicate area where conscience registers sin and where each of us is most attuned to the nuances of relationship. With this area desensitized, it is only a matter of time before our faith is also numbed. A spiritual movement of independence gathers force underground and comes out into the open, using doubt as its prime organ of propaganda.

The theme of remembering, with its twin truth of giving thanks, is inseparable from faith in the Bible. The man or woman of faith is the one who remembers, and the one who remembers is the one who gives thanks. Unbelief, on the other hand, has a short and ungrateful memory. This is true for whole nations as well as for individuals, as Israel's history proved.

Again and again as the nation prepared to cross the river Jordan and enter the Promised Land, Moses solemnly charged them: "Remember!" No one knew better than he their stubbornness and volatile fickleness, demonstrated repeatedly after the exodus from Egypt. When the people were in Egypt, they cried out for freedom, but when they were free, they cried out to go back. If there was a lack of water, they complained, and if there was water, they complained that there was no meat. There was always something else, the next thing, always "if only . . ."

At the root of all their recalcitrance lay ingratitude and a failure to remember. So, to prevent the disastrous consequences he foresaw, Moses drove home the lesson: "Remember!" They were to remember where they came from: "Remember that you were slaves in Egypt and the LORD your God brought you out with a strong hand and an outstretched arm."[7] They were to remember how they had come: "You must remember all that road by which the LORD your God has led you these forty years in the wilderness."[8] And they were warned that even in prosperity and success they were not to forget: "When you eat your fill there, be careful not to forget the LORD who brought you out of Egypt."[9] Their festivals were to be a commemoration of God's acts,[10] and even some of their clothes were to carry a reminder: "Into this tassel you shall work a violet thread, and whenever you see this in the tassel, you shall remember all the LORD's commands and obey them."[11]

But the lesson was not learned, and the checkered pattern of independence and ingratitude was repeated. In the dark days during and after the exile the lesson was reiterated with the added weight of still more history. "Our fathers in Egypt took no account of thy marvels, they did not remember thy many acts of faithful love," wrote the Psalmist. "They quickly forgot all he had done."[12] Or, as Nehemiah vividly expressed it, "They ate and were satisfied and grew fat and found delight in thy great goodness. But they were defiant and rebelled against thee."[13] This ingratitude in "forgetting to remember" is the key to the tragic failure of the chosen people. Speaking through Hosea, God himself sums up the lesson of Israel's failure: "They were filled, and, being filled, grew proud; and so they forgot me."[14]

What was possible for Israel under the Old Covenant is no less possible for the church under the New. "What do you possess that was not given you?" Paul asked the Corinthians, and the unanswerable logic of his question was designed to cut decisively at the root of ingratitude.[15] Gratitude, by contrast, changes everything. One mark of the exuberant joy of the early Christians and a secret of their costly praise was an overwhelming sense of God's grace behind the whole of life.

Focusing more particularly on forgiveness, Jesus defended the woman who had poured myrrh over his feet by pointing to the same reason: "Her great love proves that her many sins have been forgiven; where little has been forgiven, little love is shown."[16] The point is not that some have been forgiven a greater number of sins than others or that some are "worse sinners" than others but that some see their need of forgiveness and others do not. The point also is that some, more than others, remember the sins they have been forgiven and are therefore more consciously grateful. Where we forget what we have been forgiven, little love is shown.

The potential for ingratitude is never far away. Ten lepers were healed by Jesus; only one returned to express thanks. When the prodigal came home and the elder brother became jealous and self-righteous, the father's antidote for his elder son's sour grapes was a refresher course for his memory: "'My boy,' said the father, 'you are always with me, and everything I have is yours.'"[17] The king's servant, forgiven a crippling debt of millions, refused to forgive his fellow servant the debt of a few coins. By demanding payment on a trifle, he is remembering what he should have forgotten and forgetting what he should have remembered—that he himself has just been forgiven. Only such forgetfulness could allow such unforgivingness.[18]

The same lesson has been appreciated through the history of the church. Augustine recognized that Paul's words touched everything: There was nothing he had which he had not received. If this was so, then all was of grace. His description of

the Christian as "a hallelujah from head to foot" is a thumbnail
sketch of the joy and gratitude of a redeemed memory. "Let me
not tire of thanking you," he wrote, "for your mercy in rescuing
me from all my wicked ways."[19]

The same grace was a marvel to John Newton centuries
later. He was a Christian for many years but quite unable to
forget that he had been "once an infidel and libertine, a servant of slaves in Africa."[20] Out of this deep sense of the "once
and might have been" which threw the wonder of salvation
into sharp relief, he wrote the hymn, "Amazing Grace." Or
as the poet W. H. Auden expressed it simply, "Let your last
thinks all be thanks."[21]

KEEPING THE LINES OPEN

Clearly, memory for a Christian is not nostalgia or historical
reverie. It is far more profound than having a mental skill or a
better-than-average ability to recall. There is all the difference
in the world, as G. K. Chesterton pointed out, between tradition as the living faith of the dead and traditionalism as the
dead faith of the living. The redeemed memory, as it works
under God's Spirit, keeps the living awareness of the present
in line with a living awareness of the past. Thus our gratitude and thanksgiving, which are spurred by a knowledge of
the past, are linked to our faith and hope, which engage the
present and look toward the future. This gives continuity
and wholeness to the life of faith that are indispensable to its
growth and maturity.

Titian has captured this dynamic continuity in his painting *An Allegory of Prudence*. Prudence has three heads, a
youth's that looks toward the future, a mature man's that
looks at the present, and an old man's that looks back on the
past with the wisdom of experience. Titian has written over

their heads *Ex Praeterito Praesens Prudenter Agit Hi Futura Actione Deturpit* ("From the [example of] the past the man of the present acts prudently so as not to imperil the future").

The Christian life turns carefully on the boundary between the present and the past. Faith is thoroughly existential, but the believer's moment-by-moment experience is never autonomous, nor is it adrift in time, for memory serves to link it to the past. But faith is also reflective, though mere memories are never allowed to become nostalgia or remorse. The good past is joyfully remembered, and the bad past is freely forgiven.

An old Russian proverb runs, "Dwell in the past and you'll lose an eye. Forget the past and you'll lose both eyes." When we lose this balance, each of us has a tendency to consider the present moment not only as unique but as autonomous. It therefore becomes a little universe of independent reality in revolt from God and the rest of time, and able to fence itself off from the lessons of the past and the demands of the future.

The redeemed memory closely allied with truth does not allow this to happen. Rather, it acts to keep open a line of communication right through the vital terrain of the past, an important sector of the battlefield for faith. If this line to the past is not kept open, rebellion against God is much easier. Both self-sufficiency and its chief agent of propaganda—doubt—depend on a strictly censored, closely monitored view of reality. Wider reality would threaten their existence. A keen memory is disastrous to their cause, but a dull memory is their ally. In keeping open the lines to the past, the redeemed memory carries encouragement and conveys warnings and lessons to faith as faith is engaged in fighting at that front line of the battle that is the present moment.

THE CHRISTENDOM DOUBT

This first variety of doubt is a rationalization. Contrary to what the doubter says, the problem is not in the belief but in the believer. It is not in the insufficiency of truth but in the ingratitude and self-sufficiency of the truster. In essence, this doubt holds nothing against truth except that it is inconvenient. It may express itself extremely vocally and raise a wide range of objections to the truth, but these are not genuine doubts. They are part of the propaganda exercise of doubt itself. The real bone of contention is that truth is unnecessary and unwelcome rather than untrustworthy.

This doubt might be called "the Christendom doubt," for it flourishes whenever a once-consistent Christian community begins to take faith for granted. It arises whenever a Christian community becomes a cocoon or whenever Christian education becomes a well-insulated pipeline from the cradle to the grave. Christians escape not only the world but the healthy tension of living within it. Without the constant reminder of the "once and might have been," it becomes harder to resist a blasé attitude of complacency.

Many students in Christian colleges are so sheltered that they have no idea of the difference that God makes that is more than verbal. The world beyond is a matter of hearsay. This is not entirely their fault. But it means that when they doubt, what they need is not another sermon but more experience, not another answer but deeper questions. Their doubt is a result of too little involvement in the world rather than too much.

In a way, this first category is a peculiarly Protestant doubt that is best understood as a misrepresentation and abuse of freedom. The genius of the Reformation lay in the fact that human beings were made free under God. Justification "by faith alone" cut away the bureaucratic jungle of human authorities and sub-servience. But where this liberty was not balanced by responsi-bility, the Reformation made human beings so free *under* God that it was only a short step to their being free *from* God. We might say that the despair of existentialism is simply the logic of atheism, but this is true only insofar as atheism itself is the logic of ungrateful Protestantism.

Not that the leaders of the Reformation were blind to this danger. Martin Luther laid stress on the old Latin prov-erb, "Nothing ages more quickly than gratitude."[22] At times he would brood gloomily as he thought of the future course of the Reformation. "The ingratitude and the irreverence of the world terrify me. Therefore I fear that this light will not long endure."[23] Fortunately for us the spiritual and cultural vitality of the Reformation outlived Luther's estimate, but we must not ignore his warning. Why is it that movements of spiritual renewal last no longer than the third generation? Isn't it partly because we forget so soon? Isn't it true that without the accompanying "form" of the past, of which memory is a vital part, "freedom" can never be more than a fragile short-lived luxury?

REMEMBERING TO REMEMBER

At first the remedy for this doubt seems simple. The doubt may be a result of forgetting, but is the remedy only a matter of remembering? In terms of *what* happens, yes, it is just that simple. Remember honestly, remember fully and the present moment will be so vividly contrasted with the "once and might have been" that a hard heart will be melted and sealed lips broken open by praise. But in terms of *how* it happens, it is not that simple. For doubt—full-grown—is not a lapse of memory but a willful refusal to remember. How can it be made to do what it will not do?

When a person's doubt is well-developed, it needs a special confrontation, one designed to disturb complacency and strike a blow at self-sufficiency. Doubts of this type are a form of games-playing that must stop. People in doubt can choose, but their choice must be made in the full light of knowing what they are doing—disbelieving, not doubting. Gently and skillfully they must be challenged to think back and think deeply. Who is God and what difference does it make if God is not there? Where were they before they believed in God? Where would they be now apart from God? Are they merely discarding a belief or are they grieving a person?

The burden of this challenge is heavy, but the style must not be. If doubt is a moral refusal to remember, "mere reminders" will be tiresome. The doubter will never remember unless God works in his or her heart bringing a conviction of sin. So we need to pray for the doubter as much as talk; raise questions rather than make statements; use the rapier and not the sledgehammer; care for him or her rather than judge. If we lecture people in doubt with a series of reminders, their defenses will be in place. But if we jog their memory, they will see our point before they can help it.

This doubt is an example of where theological answers may be unwise because the doubter is insensitive. But whose ministry is it to bring things to mind and to convict? The Holy Spirit's, of course.[24] But it is one thing for us to know that a person needs God's conviction and another thing to say so to him or her. Praying and saying little is just as much a way of presupposing God as preaching and saying too much.

When doubt is less developed, remembering comes as prevention rather than cure. Keeping alive a grateful memory is a spiritual art. Leave it to those moments that are spontaneous and it will tend to be as transient as it is spontaneous. But structure it too heavily and the gain in increased remembering will be at the expense of a diminishing sense of personal involvement at any particular moment when we do remember. Ideally the ministry of remembering should be a bright thread running through all our Christian living—individually, corporately, publicly, privately; in the quiet moment of intimate prayer as well as in the open statements of public thanksgiving; for single people, for couples, for families, for churches, for communities, and for nations.

A lively memory is not the same thing as a colorful testimony. The latter can become a point of pride and end in denying what it set out to affirm. The redeemed memory loses all value if it is only a formal, public rehearsal. What matters is the heart and its secret whispers before God. King David shows us the way when he says, "It is good to give thanks to the LORD . . . and make thy praise our pride."[25] So long as "God's praise . . . our pride" is the attitude of our hearts, there will be no place for this kind of doubt. But as soon as we forget, just as soon as "no praise" describes the situation in our hearts, "No praise . . . self-pride" will be the result. The doubt that inevitably follows will be the press release of self-sufficiency taking over and settling in.

"My father," said the ancient Hebrews in a solemn annual declaration, "was a wandering Aramean"—and they then remembered. "Our fathers," said Governor Bradford to his fellow Puritans who landed at Plymouth, "were Englishmen who came over this great ocean, and were ready to perish in this wilderness; but they cried unto the Lord, and he heard their voyce, and looked on their adversitie" and the sons and daughters of the Pilgrims then remembered.[26] "The seat of the mind," Augustine wrote, "is in the memory."[27]

Part of the molding power of the modern world is its

ability to leave us all blasé. It makes us accustomed to the convenient, the instant, the efficient, the routine, the engineered, and the calculated. It encourages in us a complacency that takes everything for granted. This is true of the world of science and technology where the spirit of secularism has triumphed, and it is no different in the area of faith. As television's Bart Simpson put it, in his celebrated grace before a meal, "Dear God, we pay for all this ourselves, so thanks for nothing."

As followers of Christ we would do well to live by the motto, "Nothing taken for granted. Everything received with gratitude. Everything passed on with grace." We would also do well to build times to remember into the regular pattern of our lives. Do you take stock at the end of a day, a week, or a year? Do you keep some record of God's goodness to help you commemorate and celebrate? Not necessarily a journal, but perhaps a note of particular answers to prayer, special acts of guidance, amazing experiences of provision? Do you fully enter into public festivals and services for remembering—the Lord's Supper, Thanksgiving, Harvest Festival, New Year's Eve? Do you pause from time to time to thank God for the hundred and one tiny joys that make up each day?

There are endless possibilities for specific ways and moments of remembering, for lifting our hearts in praise to God. We all need to take gratitude more seriously than we do. The prophet Samuel raised a monument to God in the hour of Israel's victory and publicly declared it, "Ebenezer, 'for to this point,' he said, 'the LORD has helped us.'"[28] In the same way the moment of remembering, the time taken out for thanks, the pause for praise, will stand before God and our fellow human beings as a statement of declared trust, of radical reliance, of faith that will admit no turning back—in short, a decisive no to self-sufficiency and doubt and an emphatic yes to God.

> *You have given so much to me.*
> *Give me one thing more—a grateful heart.*
>
> —George Herbert

—■|—

CHAPTER 4

FAITH
OUT OF FOCUS

Doubt from a Faulty
View of God

Have you ever been met at an airport or a station by someone who didn't know you? Usually it is not too hard to spot the person by his broad welcoming smile or the eager, slightly nervous way he scans the arriving passengers. But once when I arrived in Boston I was at a loss. No one stepped forward, no one seemed to be on the lookout for a stranger, and the other passengers quickly dispersed. Then, just when I was wondering if there had been some mistake, a man came up full of apologies. "I'm so sorry," he said. "I completely missed you. I was expecting someone quite different!"

PICTURES AND PEOPLE

The idea we have of people always affects the way we see them. Sometimes our pictures are so inaccurate that we see them wrongly or miss them altogether. Imagine, for a moment, a rather different ending to my experience. What if the official welcomer had stuck to his preconceptions to the point of concluding that I had not arrived? In one sense, he would be right—the person he had in mind had not arrived. But in a more important sense, he would be wrong, for there is no such person as he had in mind, and I would have been there all the time.

When we speak of "the idea we have of people," we are referring to a kind of picture of them we carry in our minds. When this picture is true, the picture and the person are one, and we are hardly conscious of the picture as something separate from the person. The picture does its job by "introducing" us to the person and helping us relate to him or her. But when an idea or the picture is false, we are more conscious of it as a separate thing, for we can clearly see it as a preconception or as a prejudice. Since the picture comes between us and the person, false ideas hinder relationships rather than help them.

The pictures we have of people act as assumptions. We expect the people to be like them and presuppose it in dealing with the people themselves. This means that our pictures can affect the relationships. To an important degree, our assumptions can even determine our relationships, just as our relationships may demonstrate our assumptions. For example, if I assume a man is honest when in fact he is a rogue, he may cheat me when I trust him. But if I assume he is a rogue when in fact he is honest, I cheat myself when I do not trust him. Trust is betrayed in each case. While the two reasons may sound opposite, they both come from the same cause—a faulty assumption. The person is different from my picture of the person.

The second category of doubt is just like this. For some reason or other believers get into their heads such a wrong idea of God that it comes between them and God or between them and their trusting God. Since they do not recognize what they are doing, they blame God rather than their faulty picture, little realizing that God is not like that at all. Unable to see God as he is, they cannot trust him as they should, and doubt is the result.

Doubt of this variety stems from a deficiency at the second level of understanding, the level at which Christian presuppositions enter for the first time. The first level is reached when a person becomes aware of his or her need. That is when searching properly begins. From then on life is marked by the search for an answer that will meet the need and prove trustworthy.

Knowing this sense of need, the searcher asks two basic questions of anyone or anything that claims to be "an answer." Does it really provide the answer? And if it does, how can it be known to be true? A searcher reaches the second level of understanding when he or she is satisfied that the Christian faith answers the first of these questions. Having encountered and then examined the Christian faith, the searcher recognizes that if it is true (as it claims to be and as the third level promises to show how it can be seen to be), *it does provide the necessary answer.*

Obviously I am not thinking of "answers" as something necessarily conceptual or purely verbal, as if a Christian answer was a string of words beginning "The Christian faith says that . . ." A nineteenth-century drunkard sobbing at the penitents' bench found no less an "answer" in the cross of Christ than a twentieth-century philosopher with carefully articulated questions. Whether the need is articulated clearly and the answer given is conceptual is not our concern here. What matters at this level is that the searcher clearly understands that if the Christian faith is true, his or her need, whatever it is, is met.

Do you see how presuppositions come in? A searcher is like a man going to buy a suit. He doesn't buy the suit and then ask later if it fits and if it is what he wants. First he looks for the one that he likes or that matches his needs, then he sees if it fits. Last of all, he pays for it. In the same way the Christian faith is presupposed by a searcher *before* it is proved. In fact it is presupposed to see if it is worth proving. Searchers typically say to themselves, "*If* the Christian faith is true, what difference would it make?" And when they ask that question they are presupposing it provisionally. Not until the third level of understanding are Christian presuppositions confirmed as certain (the suit "fits"), and not until the fourth level are they accepted as final and chosen as personal (the suit is paid for; it belongs).

Don't be put off by the term "Christian presuppositions." Christian presuppositions are simply Christian truths presupposed. We could insert "Christian truths" (or doctrines or promises) for "Christian presuppositions," but I prefer to speak this way to focus attention on what a presupposition does rather than on what it is. If we said "truths," it would be easy to think of their content only. But when we say "presuppositions," the stress is not on truth's content but on truth being counted on. But, of course, the presuppositions must never remain purely abstract. Christian presuppositions are nothing less than the whole truth of who God is and what he has done for us. We are speaking here of presuppositions, but just as easily we could spell them out in terms of specific things, such as God's holiness or justice or love, or simply that "Jesus loves me."

From this second level onward, the element of presupposing will always be a part of faith. This means that presuppositions are not just a part of coming to believe but the heart of continuing to believe. A businessman may try on a suit in the fitting-room, but a suit is bought to be worn—in business. So when presuppositions are seen to fit, they are to be "assumed," that is, to be put on and worn. What matters is not the shop but the street outside and the office ahead.

To change the picture, presuppositions are not a booster

rocket to get faith off the ground—to be jettisoned as soon as faith is in orbit. They are as vital to faith as an engine to an airplane. What falls away when we believe, which distinguishes coming to faith from continuing to believe, is the "if-ness" or trial-run quality of the early use of presuppositions. Knowledge is always presuppositional, but at a certain point it is no longer provisional. Once presuppositions have been tested, found to be true and adopted, they can be counted on.

FAULTY PICTURE OF GOD

To believe in God is to "let God be God." This is the chief business of faith. As we believe we are allowing God to be in our lives what he already is in himself. In trusting God, we are living out our assumptions, putting into practice all that we say he is in theory so that who God is and what he has done can make the difference in every part of our lives.

This means that the accuracy of our pictures of God is not tested by our orthodoxy or our testimonies but by the truths we count on in real life. It is demonstrated when the heat is on, the chips are down, and reality seems to be breathing down our necks. What we presuppose at such moments is our real picture of God, and this may be very different from what we profess to believe about God.

Presuppositions, therefore, are vital to faith. They affect the picture of reality we hold in our minds, and if they are sharply or poorly focused, reality will be correspondingly clear, blurred, or distorted. As with a pair of glasses, presuppositions determine what we see and how we see it, but they do not necessarily determine what there is to be seen.

The same is true of faith in God. If we presuppose in practice what is true in fact, then our faith in God is focused clearly and our picture of God is true—that is, it allows God to be God.

But if our picture of God is wrong, then our whole presupposition of what it is possible for God to be or do is correspondingly altered. When the presuppositions are wrong, the picture is wrong. Faith is out of focus, God is not seen as he is, and in this field of badly focused vision, with its dangerous loss of clarity or completeness, doubt easily grows. Such doubts are the direct result of a faulty picture of God.

Notice exactly where the problem lies. This type of doubt is not a matter of doubting the right presuppositions but of believing the wrong ones. That is an important difference. If our presuppositions were right but we could not believe them, the problem would lie elsewhere (as we will see in Chapters 6 and 9). The problem arises here when we still believe our presuppositions even though they are wrong.

Give yourself a simple test. Think back to some crisis in your life (a moment of shock or time of stress or failure). What did your attitudes then show you of your real view of God? Or think back to some deep personal concern and the way you brought it to God in prayer. In situations like those, we see our real views of God. What faith is asking always reveals what it is assuming. What faith says in a situation is an expression of what it sees behind the situation. If it asks confidently, it is because it assumes correctly. Other motivations may pull out of line this relationship between assuming and asking, but at its purest, faith is strong or weak, advances or retreats in direct proportion to what it assumes.

If we say we believe God is there and that he loves us but live as if he were dead or couldn't care less about us, then the beliefs we presuppose in practice are out of line with the beliefs we profess in theory, and we are bound to doubt God eventually. This is why living faith is better tested in crises than in creeds, in failure rather than success. Sometimes the way we act shows up our beliefs as little better than the hazy notions of an unbeliever. One minute we are reciting the most orthodox creed and the next minute we are practicing a pathetic view of God that would do no credit to a pagan. As Oswald Chambers writes, "Faith by its very nature must be tried, and the real trial of faith is not that we find it difficult to trust God, but that God's character has to be cleared in our minds."[1]

HOW FAULTY PICTURES HAPPEN

There are two main ways in which our minds can be affected by faulty presuppositions. The first is by allowing pre-Christian presuppositions to remain after we have come to faith. Instead of rooting them out and replacing them, we can leave them undisturbed until they are intermingled with the new presuppositions of Christian truth that should be the sole foundation of the Christian's mind. Often this lingering on passes unnoticed because changes in other areas, such as lifestyle, seem so drastic and appear so obvious. A new broom has swept through everything, but the basic furnishings of the old presuppositions go untouched. The result is a sorry compromise in which the old assumptions neutralize the new ones and act as a Trojan Horse in the mind. Finally the point is reached where our minds are not renewed so much as patched up. Or worse, the old presuppositions completely usurp the place of the new.

No army would advance into enemy territory and carelessly leave behind it pockets of resistance. If it did, it would find that temporary gain in speed of advance would be more than offset by eventual loss. Likewise, our Christian thinking will make little progress unless its presuppositions are continually renewed by being brought into line with God's truth.

God's warning to the Israelites as they embarked on their conquest of the Promised Land applies to the renewal of mind we each should experience. "If you do not drive out the inhabitants of the land as you advance, any whom you leave in possession will become like a barbed hook in your eye and a thorn in your side. They shall continually dispute your possession of the land."[2] The renewed mind is nothing less than the mind of Christ in the follower of Christ, a mind so under Christ's authority that its presuppositions are entirely influenced and informed by the truth of God. Anything less or anything other than this is not only untrue but alien and unhelpful. If it is not dealt with, it will inevitably create doubts.

The second main way in which a Christian's mind can be affected is by allowing alien presuppositions to enter and dominate afterward. Usually infiltration of this sort is not obvious, or the mind would instinctively reject it. (A frog dropped into hot water will jump out instantly in a reflex action of escape.) But if the alien premises are subtle and pervasive, they can filter in and overpower the mind before it is even aware of their presence, let alone their danger. (A frog can be boiled alive in water that is brought to boil slowly.)

One example is those who come to faith today—in a highly mix-and-match era of thinking—and have their faith in Christ jumbled together with leftover bits and pieces of Buddhism and New Age ideas. A sadder example is those who have been Christians for some time but who are taken over, or perhaps taken in, by the deep relativism in modern concepts of truth. Whether this comes from false forms of tolerance that are really indifference or from more explicit dismissal of absolutes, modern relativism has a strongly corrosive effect on historic Christian conviction. It shears the historic Christian faith of its unique strength—the conviction of its claim to truth. The result is a significant number of Christians, as bewildered as they are faithful, who are left to struggle bravely with the doubts that the situation creates. Considering the relativism eating into faith today, it is hard to know which is more surprising—that so many people lose their faith or that more do not.

One reason why many people do not lose their faith is that they are protected by their lifestyles from the uncomfortable logic of the deficiency in their faith. But this is dangerous. The subtlety of the wrap-around influence of alien presuppositions is that they do their work before they are noticed. Whether it is a Christian student surrounded by relativism on a university campus or a Christian family surrounded by the influence of the mass media, too few are awake to the danger. And when they do wake up to the situation, they find that the combat against relativism is not a clean, hand-to-hand fight but a wearing war of nerves against an enemy who is everywhere and nowhere, friendly-seeming but deadly at the same time.

Whether the problem is the result of old presuppositions that have not been rooted out or of alien presuppositions that have filtered in, the effect is the same. The presuppositions are wrong, so the picture of God is wrong too. Faith is out of focus, not seeing God as he is, and temptation to doubt is inevitable. When such temptation comes, it is an amber light to warn of the worldliness of mind into which we are slipping.

Don't miss one point: If God *really were* like our picture of him, then the doubt would be valid. But it is our picture of God, not God, that is at fault, and the doubt is fueled solely by misunderstanding. Sometimes when I listen to people who say they have lost their faith, I am far less surprised than they expect. If their view of God is what they say, then it is only surprising that they did not reject it much earlier.

Other people have a concept of God so fundamentally false that it would be better for them to doubt than to remain devout. The more devout they are, the uglier their faith will become since it is based on a lie. Doubt in such a case is not only highly understandable, it is even a mark of spiritual and intellectual sensitivity to error, for their picture is not of God but an idol.

This second variety of doubt indicates that faith is suffering from a confusion of truth and error, a mixture of Christian and non-Christian presuppositions that have produced a disintegrated frame of mind. Doubts like this crystallize at one of two points, either where the presuppositions are so mixed and unsatisfactory that they are inaccurate, or where the presuppositions are true as far as they go but do not go far enough so they are incomplete. Although true, in the sense that they are not in error, the latter are not the whole truth and this is their problem. In the first instance the picture of God is at fault because it is all wrong, and in the second because it is too small.

A GOD ALL WRONG

A biblical example of the first problem can be seen in the hopeless compromise of faith produced by religious syncretism in the ninth century B.C. On entering the Promised Land, the Israelites found that every piece of the land had its own deity, its own "Baal" (meaning "lord" or "possessor"). Probably in all innocence they had begun to use the word *Baal* to describe the Lord God. But by the ninth century this practice had degenerated into gross confusion. Under its cover, the worship of Baal-Melquart, the official god of Tyre, had crept in and corrupted faith in God.

The prophet Elijah's approach to this was direct: Confront the people and clarify the issues. Was he, Elijah, the cause of the problem or was Ahab? Was Baal truly sovereign or was the Lord? The people were commanded to assemble and were faced with a simple choice: "Elijah stepped forward and said to the people, 'How long will you sit on the fence? If the LORD is God, follow him; but if Baal, then follow him.'"[3] There was to be no limping between two opinions. They were not to serve two masters. They were not to be in two minds. They were to choose, and they were to live with the consequences of their choice.

We have a similar situation today, though with different details. Faith is a drab and joyless affair to many Christians because what they presuppose is a sorry mixture of Christian and non-Christian ideas. They are half-hearted because they are double-minded. They want the best of both worlds, but they find the best of neither and the worst of each. If they are less than complete in rejecting the Christian faith, they are less than complete in believing it. One person is a Christian but carries over her previous attitude to race and wealth. Another person believes in God but still subscribes to his naturalistic view of science. With some the problem of premises is theoretical; with others it is practical.

In each case, the foreign presuppositions bring their problems with them. Believe in naturalism and you weaken your view of prayer. Believe in relativism and you won't see Christian truth as unique. Believe in dialectical materialism and the class struggle will be more important to you than the kingdom of God. Carry over the assumptions of psychological determinism and the new nature of the Christian will be reduced to a figure of speech. Carry over the assumptions of philosophical positivism and the basic notions of revelation will become nonsense. Carry over any presupposition that is not in accord with Christian truth and doubts are bound to arise.

What is the answer to this type of doubt? Once we appreciate how this doubt develops, we must be careful to presuppose only what we know to be true and to commit ourselves consciously to the consequences of these presuppositions. If certain assumptions are true, it only makes sense to demonstrate this by counting on them in practice. Equally, if we conclude that other presuppositions are not true, we can be sure that in the long run they will not prove satisfactory either, and we should root them

out. Centuries before Elijah, Joshua glimpsed the same syncretis-
tic tendencies in Israel and delivered an ultimatum to the people:
"'If it does not please you to worship the LORD, choose here and
now whom you will worship: the gods whom your forefathers
worshipped beside the Euphrates, or the gods of the Amorites in
whose land you are living. But I and my family, we will worship
the LORD.'"[4]

Put differently, true faith is always iconoclastic.
Everything in our hearts and minds that is less or other than
God must be smashed, for it is not God. As C. S. Lewis wrote,
"Images of the Holy easily become holy images—sacrosanct.
My idea of God is not a divine idea. It has to be shattered time
after time. He shatters it Himself. He is the great iconoclast."[5]
In fact, such a shattering is a mark of true prayer. "The most
blessed result of prayer would be to rise thinking 'But I never
knew before, I never dreamed . . . ' I suppose it was at such a
moment that Thomas Aquinas said of all his own theology, 'It
reminds me of straw.'"[6]

Once such a doubt has developed, the best way to deal
with it is to bring it to a head. At the point where the Christian
and the non-Christian premises are confused, the issues will
be too. But to clarify things, locate the questionable premises
and follow them through to their logical conclusion so that the
person in doubt can see it. Don't be sidetracked into answering a surface problem or comforting the person in doubt if the
alien presuppositions are left unchallenged. The way this kind
of doubt is expressed is only a symptom of the deeper problem
of premises, and there is no final remedy unless you deal with
the root cause.

When Augustine examined the thought of the heretics of
his day, his constant refrain was, "See where it leads to. . . ."[7]
Pascal argued the same way: "The hypothesis that the Apostles
were knaves is quite absurd. Follow it out to the end."[8] C. S.

Lewis's recent equivalent was "Think it out to the ruddy end."
This is the thinking believer's equivalent of Christ's statement,
"You will recognize them by their fruits."[9] What the seed is to
the fruit, the premise is to the conclusion. Many of us might
never be able to distinguish one variety of seed from another,
but we have no trouble in telling an apple from a pear or a
cauliflower from a cabbage.

The same is true of presuppositions and conclusions. Find
out what people in doubt are believing wrongly and help them
follow the logic of these presuppositions to their necessary conclusion. Challenge them to check the full-blown consequences
of their ideas to see where they lead. They will then see that
their views are both wrong and unchristian. Nothing is more
nourishing to doubt than hazy mists of vagueness, but clear
thinking disperses mist and leaves a clear-cut choice to believe
or to disbelieve.

A GOD TOO SMALL

The second problem—having inadequate, as distinct from inaccurate, presuppositions—is different but just as dangerous. The
weakness here is that the assumptions are incomplete rather
than incorrect. But the effect is the same. In the long run they are
incorrect to the degree that they are incomplete.

Part of the purpose of faith is to help us make sense of life
as we experience it. So if we adopt presuppositions that are too
small to handle the reality we are facing, their rationality and
coherence will be equally cramped.

If we believe in God, yet at the same time presuppose a
picture of God that is less than he is, our faith is bound to suffer. Our conception of God will be pinched and uncomfortable.
The false idea of God will act like a tight collar on faith, throt-
tling its style, confining its movements, shutting down the full

freedom of truth. Could someone expect to be comfortable if he is wearing a belt two inches too tight or a pair of shoes two sizes too small? Is it different for faith? Confronted with a shrunken picture of God, faith has no room to be itself and doubt is the expression of its discomfort.

Sarah's reaction to the news that she would give birth to a son in her old age is a good example. She knew that her husband was past it and that she herself was beyond the age of childbearing, so her first reaction was to laugh. But God confronted her about that laugh—not because she laughed in God's presence but because her laughter expressed a limiting view of God that was a denial of his power and an incitement to doubt. "The LORD said to Abraham, 'Why did Sarah laugh and say "Shall I indeed bear a child when I am old?" Is anything impossible for the LORD?'"[10] Sarah laughed at God's promise because she doubted that it was possible, and she doubted it was possible because her conception of God was too small.

The same problem of shrunken faith showed up in the attitudes of many who approached Jesus for help. Very few came with a complete understanding of who he was, so their faith was correspondingly weak.

A leper once begged Jesus for help: "'If only you will,' said the man, 'you can cleanse me.'"[11] The father of the demented son pleaded, "But if it is at all possible for you, take pity upon us and help us."[12] Notice the difference in each appeal. The leper saw no problem in trusting Jesus' power—it was Jesus' compassion he was unsure of. His appeal could be expressed, "I know you could if you would, but you probably won't." The father, on the other hand, was unsure of Jesus' power, and it is almost as if he says, "I know you would if you could, but you probably can't."

The response Jesus gave to each of them is fascinating. To the leper, who sensed his power but not his love, "Jesus stretched out his hand [and] touched him."[13] But to the father who had little sense of his divine power, he replied, "'If it is possible!' . . . Everything is possible to one who has faith."[14] Each had an incomplete faith because the aspect of truth he sensed was only a part of the full truth of who Jesus is. So Jesus concentrated on the part that needed filling out if faith was to be itself.

What is the answer to this second error? Simply to correct the picture, the presuppositions. They need stretching and filling out so that they reflect the fullness and adequacy of who God is. This is not a theoretical or mechanical exercise. It must be personal, and it must be specific. *We* must do the work, and we must do it *where it is needed.* If I see God's power clearly but not his wisdom, then it is no use my finding out about his justice or faithfulness. What I need to know is his wisdom, and this means wrestling with the truth of it until I can count on it myself.

This is not our work alone. God has revealed himself through his Spirit in his Word, and he continues to do so. Moreover, God is bigger to us than our small ideas of him and more gracious to us than our mean views of who he is. He is more eager and able to expand our faith than we are to do it. We are all more shortsighted than we realize, but there is no one who cannot count on the illuminating power of the Holy Spirit.

Putting it this simply does not make light of the doubt. It takes seriously the fact that, with these given presuppositions, it is little wonder that there is some doubt, and this is only the beginning of it. *But again, the presuppositions that produce such doubts do not describe God, for the god they describe is not God.* How often we cramp faith and insult God by entertaining puny conceptions of him. How many times God must be saying to us what he said in anticipating Israel's doubts after the exile:

"Even if it may seem impossible to the survivors of this nation
on that day, will it also seem impossible to me?"[15]

TWO SUBTLETIES IN HANDLING DOUBT

This is a useful place to note two things that are also true of the
other categories of doubt. First, this type of doubt can easily
be part of a "compound" doubt. The immediate cause may be
theological—presuppositions that are inaccurate or inadequate,
but this is not necessarily the root of the problem. How did
these faulty presuppositions get there in the first place? Trace the
answer to that and it may lead into much deeper waters, such as
past history and psychological factors.

Take, for example, two people who have a problem realizing that God really loves them, so that mention of God's holiness inspires only anxiety or guilt. For both of them their doubt
has become a protective reflex against the unhealthy responses
they feel forced to make to such a God. But *why* do they see God
like that? That is the real question. For one of them, the reason
may lie no deeper than an ignorance of who God is, with all his
Father's love as the Bible and Jesus reveal him. Whereas for the
other, his faulty picture may go back to badly tangled family
relationships that have left him unable to see any authority as
good or loving.

Both of them carry over this faulty picture into their relationship with God, though for different reasons. The first person
has been wrongly taught and the second wrongly treated. This
means that for the first one, the doubt is "simple" and can be
cleared up in a straightforward way, but for the second, it is
"compound" and needs much greater care. Any counsel that
tackles only the surface expression of the doubt lacks compassion and is bound to fail. (We will look at these psychologically
grounded doubts in more detail in Chapter 9.)

Second, as with the remedy for most doubts, there are two parts to approaching it. The short-term need is to deal with the roots of the doubt—in this case, a matter of the incompleteness of the doubter's picture of God—while the long-term need is to train a habit of faith that will close the door to this type of doubt in the future.

In terms of the doubt we are discussing, the long-term habit of faith is particularly important because the constant drive of our fallen natures is toward idolatry. The principle of sin leads to the perspective of sin. The claim to the right for myself leads to an insistence on viewing all reality from my viewpoint alone. In our sin, we therefore reduce God to our human image, scale him down to our size, and substitute our view of God for God himself. Once this happens, it is no longer God who is over us, judging us by his Word, but we who are over God, using our god-concepts to justify what we are doing and to make judgments on what he should be doing.

"Let God be God" and we are on the path of discipleship. But let smaller pictures of God satisfy us and squeeze him out, and we are back on the easier road to cheap grace and nominal faith. The latter is the respectable person's introduction to idolatry. We love our idols because we made them. God's truth, however, is much less comfortable, and the habit of being stretched by its demands is challenging. But the rewards are incomparable, for we have the joy of getting to know God for himself, with the attached strings of lesser motives cut away.

What picture of God do you show in your beliefs? Is it sharp and clear or blurred and ill-defined? Is it something you have dreamed up? Or stuck together from various descriptions like an identikit picture? Or is it the picture God has given us of himself? Is it complete and whole? Or is part of it missing so that you trust what you know but wonder what the rest is like?

If we make sure of the right answer to these questions, we

will develop the full, clear picture of God that he himself has given us in his revelation. If we content ourselves with anything less, we can only expect to doubt. In this sense, there is a prayer that precedes all prayer:

> *May it be the real I who speaks.*
> *May it be the real Thou that I speak to.*
>   —C. S. Lewis

CHAPTER 5
————■|————

NO REASON
WHY NOT

Doubt from
Weak Foundations

I remember a student who dropped into our home some years ago on his way around Europe. Almost immediately he began to share with us the intense enthusiasm of his newfound faith in Christ. After listening for some time, I began to grow uneasy. I felt suspicious that his faith, though enthusiastic, was almost entirely groundless. Eventually I asked him how he had become a Christian and why he had believed, and then asked him how he would answer some of the questions that his forthcoming semester at a French university was bound to raise.

Finally, with considerable reluctance, I warned him that his faith seemed to have very little foundation. And that unless he had more understanding to match his enthusiasm, he was in danger of being tripped by the questions of life—not to speak of his fellow students. He listened politely, and if he showed no concern, at least he took no offense and we parted on good terms.

Within a month I received a letter, short and to the point. "I am writing to tell you that I no longer believe in God or consider myself a Christian." And then after a brief explanation, "The only reason I write to you is that you warned me this would happen." This is a clear example of the third kind of doubt, a doubt that is one of the commonest in the twentieth-century. For every person who experiences what this student did, countless others are potentially as vulnerable. It is only their sheltered lives that keep them from facing the same problem.

THE BURNING QUESTION OF TRUTH

The third type of doubt stems from a simple but basic deficiency in understanding why the Christian faith is true. This is the issue at stake in the third level of understanding. The importance of this level can hardly be exaggerated today. I can't emphasize the point too often: understanding Christians know not only *what* they believe but *why* they believe. They are able to say that what they believe is true, and behind such a statement they have sure and sufficient reasons of which they are fully persuaded.

Strong rational foundations for faith are the third level of understanding in faith. When someone has faced the critical nature of his or her dilemma without God (the first level) and has come to recognize that *if* God's revelation is true there is a meaningful answer to their dilemma (the second level), then the next urgent question is: But how do I know God's revelation is *true*?

If the searcher finds no answer to that question or if the question is not encouraged (or still worse, not allowed), then the searcher may become a believer, but he or she will be constantly at the mercy of the potential doubt that faith is only make-believe. He or she will never be certain that it is not a form of psychological wish-fulfillment and that belief in God is not purely a result of need for God—a faith for foxholes, a God of the gaps, a crutch.

This doubt is far from new, but today's intellectual climate provides an ideal breeding ground, and it has come into its own again. It is a very damaging doubt and needs to be blocked firmly by a decisive reaffirmation of what it means that the Christian faith is true.

The Christian faith is not true because it works. It works because it is true. No issue is so fundamental both to the searcher and to the believer as the question of truth. The uniqueness and trustworthiness of the Christian faith rest entirely on its claim to be the truth. God, who is the Father of Jesus Christ, is either there or he is not there. Either he has spoken or he has not spoken. What his revelation claims is either true or false. Jesus either rose from the dead or he didn't. There are no two ways about it.

This stubborn insistence on truth is one thing that lifts the Christian faith out of the common pool of completely personal, relativistic, subjective beliefs. As a young Christian exclaimed to me rather oddly on realizing for the first time the titanic implications of this claim, "I always knew the Christian faith was true, but I never realized it was *this* true!"

Naturally the stronger the claims to truth that we make for the Christian faith, the stronger our substantiation must be. The Christian faith is not true because it makes its claims more boldly or more loudly than anything else (or belief would be taken over by bravado). If it claims to be true, it must be willing to show the areas in which the evidence for its claims can be examined and found to be true. At this point the Christian faith is not only willing, it is eager. How this process of confirmation is carried out is a question that would take us beyond our immediate purpose. What matters at this point is to see the importance for faith and doubt that this claim implies.[1]

This at least should be clear: The Christian faith invites people to an examined faith. Although we Christians should believe simply, we should not "simply believe." For one thing, the pale brand of modern faith that lapses into "easy believism" has little in common with the virile attitude of understanding-plus-commitment that is the biblical notion of faith.

Higher still, there is a real danger in what both Coleridge and Tolstoy warned against: those who love "Christianity better than truth."[2] Peter Berger gives the reason. Arguments for faith that use criteria other than truth in dealing with questions of truth are forms of bad faith. "Whatever religious propositions we take, we confront thereby a burning question of truth. 'God exists'—yes or no? Is the statement true or is it not? No other criterion but that of truth respects the dignity of such a proposition."[3]

But highest of all, God is truth, so no one who is casual about truth can claim to be a true lover of God or Christ. At this point many Christians in America are casual about truth to the point of shame. Compare such neglect to Augustine's passion for truth that was nothing less than his soul's passion for God. He compared it to a voracious appetite and attributed it to his mother Monica's prayers: "It is by your prayers—I know it and admit it without hesitation—that God has given me a mind to place the Discovery of Truth above all things, to wish for nothing else, to think of nothing else, to love nothing else."[4]

Is truth merely a brittle recitation of facts? A sterile compliance with logic? Far from it. Passion for truth is passion for God. No wonder our Christian responsibility is to understand and be able to express what we believe and why. Or, as the Apostle Peter expressed it, "Be always ready with your defence whenever you are called to account for the hope that is in you."[5] If you hear someone claiming to believe something but even after listening carefully it never becomes clear exactly what he or she believes or why, you are surely entitled to wonder if the belief is valid at all. Unless our Christian faith includes this level of understanding, we are short-changing ourselves.

KNOW WHY AND KNOW WHERE

Two qualifications should be quickly added. I am not saying that someone who does not understand faith has no faith. Large numbers of people become followers of Christ for all sorts of reasons other than the fact that they fully understand why the Christian faith is true. Undeniably their faith is genuine, but the weakness is that their faith is developed at the expense of their understanding. This may be preferable to the opposite mistake (where someone's understanding is far stronger than his or her faith), but a better way is to develop both faith and understanding together.

We can become Christians for all sorts of reasons. But if the Christian faith *is* true, it is vital that we think through our faith afterward to the point where we understand why we believe—at least to the level our minds demand satisfaction in other areas of life. We should know why we believe.

A second qualification must be added. We may have sure and sufficient reasons for coming to believe, but we won't always have similar substantiation in every field. The Christian faith is rational partly because it is a faith with a foundation of sure and sufficient reasons. But it is one thing to have sufficient understanding in coming to believe and another to have it in every area of continuing to believe. We should know where we can understand and where we can't.

People often misunderstand the rationality of faith. They imagine that they have believed in God because faith is rational—which it is. But they then expect every aspect of faith to be equally open to rational investigation—which it isn't. So when they come across the first mystery they can't understand, they conclude that the Christian faith is irrational after all. God has led them to believe it was rational, but now apparently he has cheated them by unfairly slipping in a mystery.

What they forget is that rationality is opposed to absurdity, not to mystery. The rationality of faith goes hand in hand with the mystery of faith. It isn't that God has hoodwinked us into believing, as if rationality were the bait and mystery the hook. Far from it. The fact is that the greatest mystery of all—the Incarnation—comes at the very beginning and is the central reason why we believe in God. We cannot explain it: That is the beginning of the mystery of faith. But because of the evidence neither can we explain it away: That is the beginning of the rationality of faith.

So there are times (as we shall see in the later chapter on suffering) when we must hold the rationality of faith together with the mystery of faith. But if we have sufficient reason for our faith, we can avoid the otherwise powerful down tow toward nonsense and absurdity.

Again, rationality is the alternative to absurdity, but it has no quarrel with mystery. Mystery is beyond human reason, but it is not against reason. It is a mystery only to us and not to God. Where God has spoken and spoken clearly, rationality comes into its own; where God has not spoken, or for his own reasons has not spoken clearly, there is the area of mystery. An area of mystery is rational to God, but our faith must suspend judgment and not press human reason to answer questions when it has insufficient information.

NO REASONS FOR FAITH

This third category of doubt strikes at the point where a Christian is strong in faith but weak in faith's foundations. What the believer assumes is correct, but it is unsupported. He or she believes all the right things but for no reasons at all or even for the wrong reasons. What happens then is not surprising. Faith runs up against an awkward question or a scornful dismissal, and suddenly everything that had seemed so unmistakably certain, meaningful, true collapses like a balloon, leaving the remnants of faith limp and deflated.

The cause is easy to see—faith had no sure and sufficient reasons. The believer is not at all certain why he or she believed. If there is "no reason why" in terms of faith, there will certainly be "no reason why not" in terms of doubt. Here precisely is the rub. As the flaw is exposed and the doubt sweeps in with its impressive academic credentials and powerful, emotional threat, the doubt is unanswerable, because there is *no reason why not.*

A celebrated example is Winston Churchill's loss of faith as a young man in India. Finding himself with time on his hands, he ordered books from England and, while others slept during the long, hot afternoons, he read voraciously—Plato, Aristotle, Macaulay, Gibbon, Darwin, and so on. Lecky's *Rise and Influence of Rationalism* particularly disturbed him. He felt he had been deceived by the ministers of his youth and passed through what he describes as a "violent and aggressive anti-religious phase which, had it lasted, might easily have made me a nuisance."[6]

The good news in his story is that Churchill returned to faith. The bad news is that his return again bypassed the mind. His faith came back as a sense of "special protection" he sought and experienced under enemy fire. "I therefore acted in accordance with my feelings," he said, "without troubling to square such conduct with the conclusions of thought."[7]

Churchill was described by one observer as "thinking with his heart" and by another as "feeling with his mind." But for lesser mortals, like most of us, this creates problems if there is a deficiency of truth in our faith. This doubt is especially prevalent today because Christian faith is often viewed as anything but a matter of truth. In the discussion of faith, truth is not even on the agenda. It is the forgotten issue. So instead of presenting a strong, clear answer to this problem, many Christians find their defenses are down at the very place where modern unbelief is most devastating. Failure to understand the significance of truth is the Achilles' heel of many Christians. The real wonder is not that some fall away after believing for so long but that some last as long as they do with as little as they have.

Any Christian in touch with thinking people outside the church must be saddened by the large numbers of people who claim to have "lost their faith." In my experience, many of them lacked little in terms of orthodoxy or experience but never understood why their faith was true. Caught with neither a foundation nor a framework for their faith, they found university-level questions puncturing their Sunday-school-level faith. Overtaxed by questions they were discouraged from facing, they escaped the tension by "graduating" from such a faith with relief.

For many Christians, the world of faith is suspended in uneasy limbo between complete ignorance (which is no longer possible) and sufficient understanding (which is not yet attained). There are those on the fringes of the church who do not really believe but have no idea why they disbelieve; there are others inside the church who do not really disbelieve but have no idea why they believe. When not pressed too hard, the former prefer to disbelieve rather than believe and the latter to believe rather than disbelieve. But both feel extremely uncomfortable if their position is tested. Tolstoy's Levin is an example of the former:

> Like the majority of his contemporaries, Levin found himself in the vaguest position in regard to religion. Believe he could not, and at the same time he had no firm conviction that all was untrue. And so, unable either to believe in the significance of what he was doing or to regard it with indifference as an empty formality, all the time he was preparing for the sacrament he was conscious of a feeling of discomfort and shame in taking part in something he did not understand, which was therefore, an inner voice told him, deceitful and wrong of him.[8]

Many Christians are examples of the latter. In each case, a lack of understanding constitutes the inauthenticity of either the faith or the doubt.

We should all examine the foundations of our faith. Why do we believe God is there? Why do we believe God is good? How do we know Jesus ever lived? How do we know Jesus rose from the dead? Why do we trust the authority of the Bible? How do we understand that the Christian faith is true? How would we answer a modern philosopher, a Freudian psychologist, the follower of an Indian guru, each of whom denies the truth of the Christian faith in a different way? Strong answers to such questions are no substitute for faith. But without strong answers, faith may be no match for doubt.

Different aspects of basic understanding are needed in different areas of the world. People in Western Europe, for example, rarely dispute that Jesus lived, but in parts of the world, the denial of his historical existence is still a canon of Marxist dogma. Different stages of our lives need different levels of comprehension to match our growth and maturity. How sad it is when believers in their forties or fifties are merely absentee landlords, living idly off the intellectual rent from the thinking of their student days. The challenges to faith will go on and must go on being answered. As we face the issues and questions before each of us *now*, do we know why we believe? Are we able to relate and apply faith to life without suppressing questions and without unnerving our security?

INVITATION TO IRRATIONALITY?

This sense of knowing for sure is a central element of biblical faith. It has been an unmistakable part of the testimony of Christian believers throughout history. But the same cannot be said of twentieth-century Christians, which is why this type of doubt is so prevalent. Modern faith suffers from a severe short-age of understanding in its basic diet, a deficiency that can be detected at many points.

One example is the place given to irrationality in faith. Take a sampling of modern preaching, such as a minister who is culturally aware or an evangelist in the classic nineteenth-century tradition. Both, in their different ways, will give impressive witness to the importance of faith, but both may have a care-less disregard for the foundations of faith. Faith's value, some even suggest, grows in direct proportion to its lack of a rational basis. Whether it is one side's cry of the "radical uncertainty" of authentic faith or the other side's reiteration of the "leap of faith," we are offered an imposing edifice of faith with little or no mention of foundations.

A whole armory of exegesis accompanies this mentality, one side often majoring on the sacrifice of Isaac in Genesis 22 and the other side on Thomas's doubt in John 20. But the best answer to the unwarranted interpretations wrested from these texts is a closer look at the very biblical passages in question.

Abraham's story is widely used to justify the irrationality of faith. Certainly his trust in God despite the opposing evidence of immediate reality was such that his faith was "counted . . . to him as righteousness."[9] But it is wrong to conclude that Abraham was commended because he trusted God for no reason whatever. Certainly, as Abraham set out to sacrifice Isaac as God had told him, his faith was flying blind. Just as it had when he set out from Ur for a country he had never seen. But as to why he knew God and obeyed him at all, Abraham's faith was not the least blind.

Quite the contrary. It is precisely because Abraham knew God that he knew he could trust God in the dark. More pre-cisely still, it was because Abraham was not in the dark about God that he could walk in the dark about Isaac. His faith was against sight, but not against reason. In terms of the immediate situation, Abraham did not know why, but in terms of the ultimate context of his life, *he knew why he trusted God who knew why*. Knowing God as he did, his faith was a trust in the face of mystery but not in the face of absurdity.

Significantly, after the mention that God had counted Abraham's faith as righteousness, Abraham's first recorded words were "O LORD God, how can I be sure?"[10] God answers this question without any hint of rebuke in a covenant promise that speaks directly to this question: "Know this for certain."[11] Abraham's faith went far beyond the reach of understanding, but it is a travesty of the facts to ignore the elements of understanding that enabled him to do so.

Another much misrepresented passage is the account of Christ's rebuke to Thomas: "Because you have seen me you have found faith. Happy are they who never saw me and yet have found faith."[12] Certainly Thomas was rebuked, but the question is why. Thomas was rebuked not because he refused to believe without enough reasons, but because he refused to believe with more than enough reasons. For three years he had been with Jesus and heard his teaching that he was bound to suffer, to die, and to be raised from the dead. So his lack of faith was not a matter of failing to straddle an impossible credibility gap but of balking at a simple step of trust on the evidence of inescapable reasons.

For Thomas to demand further evidence at that stage was doubly unnecessary. Not only had he heard the words of Christ, he had listened to the eyewitness accounts of his fellow disciples. Yet still he refused to believe. Those who misuse this passage to encourage a "leap of faith" also ignore the fact that Jesus still invited him to touch and see. It was unnecessary, but if that was what it would take for Thomas to believe, then even that was possible. Fortunately for Thomas's self-respect, the sheer excess of grace as well as evidence made further proof unnecessary.

JUST AS JESUS SAID

The biblical view of knowledge has many dimensions. Some of them go far beyond a knowing that is solely related to reasons, but "reason-able" knowledge is a basic part of knowing in the Bible. Biblically, much of what is knowable can be checked, verified, substantiated, and confirmed.

The Gospel of John tells of the royal officer who returns home to discover that his son has recovered: "The father noted [knew] that this was the exact time when Jesus had said to him, 'Your son will live,' and he and all his household became believers."[13] The officer believed in Jesus, and an essential part of his coming to faith rested on the exact correspondence he observed between what Jesus had said and what had happened.

Luke brings out this same point in describing the reaction of the Berean Jews as they heard the gospel for the first time. "They received the message with great eagerness, studying the scriptures every day to see whether it was as they said. Many of them therefore became believers."[14] And the point is put beyond dispute in the careful declaration of purpose in John's Gospel, expressly written about the evidence of Christ's signs: "There were indeed many other signs that Jesus performed in the presence of his disciples, which are not recorded in this book. Those here written have been recorded in order that you may hold the faith [or, that you may come to believe] that Jesus is the Christ, the Son of God."[15]

The force of the evidence is plain. Faith is an act of the whole person, not of the understanding alone. But it is precisely because it is an act of the whole person that it includes the understanding. As we progress in our faith, we will be led into areas "beyond reason." But what we mean by this is beyond *humanly discernible* reasons and not in any sense *against* reason. So Christians who glory in the nonrational basis of faith leave themselves vulnerable to a lethal blow that strikes at the foundation of faith. The only comfort is to remember that it is foreseeable and quite unnecessary.

A second place to witness today's deficiency of understanding is in the improper place given to experience at the expense of understanding. Many Christians are afraid of rationalism and rightly suspicious of a purely intellectual faith. What they forget, though, is that if knowledge-without-experience is a product of rationalism, so also is experience-without-knowledge. Yet they reject the first and welcome the second. Knowledge-without-experience is only the reverse side of the coin of experience-without-knowledge. Both are born of rationalism, and both are equally wrong and finally destructive of true faith. To come to faith on the basis of experience alone is unwise, though not so foolish as to reject faith altogether because of lack of experience.

The biblical relationship of understanding to experience is quite different. Knowledge and experience are not opposed but related, and there is a profound spiritual logic in the relationship. Experience does not generate itself. Nor is it self-justifying and self-sustaining. Instead, the quality of our Christian experience depends on the quality of our faith, just as the quality of our faith depends on the quality of our understanding of God's truth.

Genuine understanding generates genuine faith, and genuine faith in turn generates genuine experience. Without genuine faith, experience can be easily counterfeited by emotionalism. Without genuine understanding, what passes for faith can be a counterfeit confidence of purely human origins (such as the power of positive thinking). So understanding is integral to faith, just as faith and understanding are both integral to experience.

In short, to deny and stifle the understanding unnecessarily is to sow a crop of future doubts. We may efface the intellect in our teaching or in our practice, but we cannot escape the uneasy conscience of a good mind trying to adapt to a bad faith. Such a mind may become so restless and frustrated with repression that sooner or later it will tear itself on some nail of its own making.

Where God has given us sure and sufficient reasons for believing, or the possibility of profound understanding in our believing, it is perverse to insist on having less than he offers. It is one thing to realize that our faith will always be weaker than we would like it to be. It is quite another to insist that our faith must be weaker than it can afford to be.

FINDING OUT FOR OURSELVES

What is the remedy for this type of doubt? First, to diagnose it correctly; second, to locate exactly where the weakness in understanding is; and third, to do the necessary homework on it, that is, to examine the matter to see what the truth of the situation is.

Are the foundations of our faith so shaky that nothing of any weight can be built on them? Or is it that because of ignorance and haste crucial parts of our foundations have been left out? This is the crux of it: Do we have good and sufficient reasons to believe what we need to believe or is our faith on shaky ground? This straightforward approach is the natural response to a situation of uncertainty, and it is also the biblical one. The attitude of the Bereans is the pattern for us all. They studied "to see whether it was as they said." When we are not sure, it is time to make sure—to see if the things that we believe are in fact true.

When the disciples first heard from the women that Jesus had risen, they were incredulous: "The story appeared to them to be nonsense, and they would not believe them."[16] But they did not stop there. Doubt was only their first reaction. It is characteristic of faith that it cannot remain in two minds; it cannot leave things in the air. Luke's next words are typical of faith's inherent drive for resolution: "Peter, however, got up and ran to the tomb, and, peering in, saw the wrappings."[17] Faith may not always know, but it always wants to know what it may. It cannot be sure of everything, but it will always be as sure as it can be. Where it is not certain, it will always seek to ascertain.

Faith does not feed on thin air but on facts. Its instinct is to root itself in truth, to earth itself in reality, and this distinguishes faith from fantasy, the object of faith from a figment of the imagination. In those places where there is a delay in confirmation, faith is prepared to wait for a long time at the bar of history. But the verdict it looks for is always the judgment of truth, the verdict handed down by reality.

Luke writes of the natural hesitancy of the Jewish believers over the unprecedented inclusion of Gentiles in the early church. But he points out that what decided the issue was Peter's laying before them the irrefutable facts of the matter so that "when they heard this their doubts were silenced."[18] This is always the way. This type of doubt is silenced by facts, answered by truth and reassured by understanding.

This insistence on knowing for sure and examining the facts of the matter is particularly important in dealing with the doubts that arise from misrepresentations of the Christian faith today. Every generation is apt to see Christ in its own image and produce its own "plastic Christ," a picture of Jesus pressed through the sieve of its own assumptions and set solidly in the mold of its own values. But it is ironic that a generation that is so impatient with the cultural adaptations of other generations has been so adept at setting up its own.

Our generation dismisses the penitential Jesus of the Middle Ages or the gentlemanly Jesus of the Victorian drawing rooms, but the selection of "Christs" offered today is worthy of the supermarket age—Jesus the Liberator, Jesus the Soul Man, Jesus the Blessed Master, Jesus the revolutionary, Jesus the archetypal poor man, Jesus the Great Prophet.

The array is bewildering and the effect is numbing. After all, how do we know that our own picture of Jesus is right, especially when we realize that we too bring assumptions to faith? Perhaps we are more shortsighted than we think? Perhaps what we believe today is no better than the Sunday school notions we were forced to discard yesterday? Perhaps it is meaningful to us only because we are believing it today? Will today's faith look as embarrassing if we look back on it tomorrow?

The train of thought that begins like this is as slippery as an eel, and the only effective way to catch it is to examine the truth of the matter. This is the only test—to unleash doubt on doubts, to examine the matter and to see where the truth lies. The trouble with most of the "modern Christs" is not that they are anti-Christian but that they are unhistorical. Our basic quarrel with them is not that they are unappealing but that they are untrue.

Do the Dead Sea Scrolls explain away the uniqueness of Jesus? Was Jesus really only a psychedelic mushroom? Is Pasolini's *The Gospel According to St. Matthew* closer to the original than the Jesus of the Christian church? Was Jesus speaking of the *Tat Tvam Asi* (Thou art That) of the Hindus when he said, "The kingdom of God is within you"?[19] Why is it that *Jesus Christ Superstar* leaves a Christian feeling so sad and angry?

Truth is the only sufficient answer faith can give that type of doubt, for it is the truth of the matter, the facts of the case that give faith its solid foundation. If faith is caught without the credentials that truth alone supplies, it knows it will be mistaken for fantasy or for wish fulfillment. It may even be tempted to wonder itself.

Some Christians think that having reasons for faith is an insult to God, as if we were desperately grubbing around for makeshift reasons to believe in him. But the opposite is the case.

Verification is only one aspect of Christian truth, but it witnesses to the unchanging authority and stability of the Word of God. We are not insulting God but bringing glory to him by taking his Word as the stable, authoritative truth it is.

Theological answers are necessary and entirely appropriate to this doubt, but they must be specific. If someone is doubting the resurrection, it is irrelevant to assure him of Christ's promise never to leave him—Christ never was with him if he has not risen. Equally, if someone has lost his sense of Christ's presence, he will need more than bare historical facts with which to rediscover it. The assurance and inner witness of the Holy Spirit are what he needs.

Here then is the third category, doubt caused by an unnecessary lack of understanding of what our faith is grounded on. If there is "no reason why" for faith, the time may come when there is "no reason why not" for doubt. And the best remedy for this doubt is to know the sure and sufficient reasons God has given us, to know why we can know God is there, to know why we can trust his revelation as true, to know why we can be sure of his love and his goodness, and to stand firm in our understanding of these truths.

ONE FOR THE BOOKS

Notice two final things about this doubt. First, as with the previous two categories, doubt of this kind may well be simple or compound. For example, someone can have a specific doubt about God that is caused by an unnecessary lack of understanding. If the doubt is simple, it can be cleared up by supplying the necessary understanding. But if the doubt is compound, you will find that a doubter can understand the answer, but he or she may be reluctant to accept it. (We will deal with this in Chapter 9.) The doubter may even refuse to search for any answer at all, though expressing the deepest need for one. This indicates a far deeper problem of which the surface doubts are only a symptom.

I can think of some doubters who keenly desired a rational faith. You could almost see them hold their breath when it dawned on them that the Christian faith is true. But then they hesitated in doubt, not because they spotted a new snag about believing but because they remembered a previous experience. Once before they had gone ahead and believed, but it had been a leap of faith with no questions asked and they fell and were hurt. This time around it is a case of "once bitten, twice shy." Their doubts were not simple but compound.

A compound doubt must be approached with special sensitivity. To people with a simple doubt, a helpful discussion, a suggested book, or a more detailed explanation may be enough to show the way along which they can eagerly search for themselves. But to people with a compound doubt, an answer that would satisfy the surface doubt alone may put even more pressure on the deeper problem and twist the knife in their hidden wounds. Providing an answer only for the surface doubt answers neither doubt in the long run.

Second, of all the families of doubt, this is probably the one best helped by reading. Not all doubts are helped by books. Some are made worse. But there is nothing like a carefully chosen book to stimulate the examination and reflection that resolves this doubt. The question "Have you thought through the basis of your faith?" is for many people almost inseparable from the best books they have read dealing with the heart of faith and understanding.

Are you building up a small library of essential books? Do you read as widely in the great classics of the faith as among modern authors? Naturally your selection will reflect your own pilgrimage, your own struggles and interests. But this will make it richer and more real when you recommend books to others who are questioning and searching.

I need add little recommendation to some of the books in my own library. Their well-thumbed, much handled appearance says it all. Scores of people have been through them, and their marginal jottings and exclamations are reminders of those who searched and those who found. Like the faith for which they argue, the best books are not there to collect dust but to stretch minds and to shed light.

AN UNSIGNED CONTRACT

Doubt from
Lack of Commitment

Afriend once told me that she no longer called herself a Christian. She wasn't at all defensive. She had no quarrel with the Christian faith or the church, and she expressed no particular doubts except that Christian things generally were rather unreal to her. After a while she shrugged her shoulders and said, "You know, I don't think I was ever really committed to Christianity."

My reply was blunt: "But do you think you have ever been really committed to anything?"

In this case, my candor was not a stab in the back or a shot in the dark; I knew her well. If there was a recurring weakness in her life, it centered around her fear to commit herself. Because of that, she rarely enjoyed anything in depth or stuck at anything for very long. Nothing ever seemed real or deeply satisfying to her.

This is an example of doubt that comes from a deficiency at the fourth level of understanding, the one that actually overlaps with the experience of becoming a Christian. Is it possible for a person to have moved through the first three levels of understanding and still leave out something essential? Can believers know their needs, know that if the Christian faith is true, it provides an answer, know on the basis of sufficient evidence that the Christian faith is in fact true, and still believe inadequately? The answer is yes—if there is a weakness in commitment.

The fourth level of understanding centers on the question of commitment. Searchers become believers when they choose and commit themselves to the consequences of their choice. This commitment is not a separate, independent stage but a higher level that builds logically on the implications of the previous levels. Like cement, an understanding commitment transforms mere beliefs into solid convictions. By *conviction* I am not suggesting the idea of "conviction of sin" but of "the courage of one's convictions."

The goal of this chapter is to examine the place of commitment and conviction in faith and thus to understand the doubt that grows out of a deficiency at the threshold of conversion. Christian conversion is rich in multi-dimensional truths and can be viewed from many angles. The modern tendency to reduce it to simplistic stereotyped formulas is an insult to the sovereign freedom of God and the integrity of human beings. Christ is the only way to God, but there are as many ways to Christ as there are people who come to him. Conversion may be gradual or sudden, quiet or dramatic, unmistakably evident to others or almost unnoticed. The variations are infinite.

Nonetheless, certain things should be present in an adequate account of conversion, and if we ignore them, we leave openings for later doubts. The individual's responsibility in conversion is to repent and believe; God's initiative and response are his gift of three things: faith, forgiveness, and the Holy Spirit; and the church's role is to welcome the new believer into the fellowship of the community of faith, symbolizing this publicly in the act of baptism.

Each of these aspects has its place as a foundation for faith, though the church's part is not so much essential to faith as an expression of faith. A weakness in any of them does not mean that faith is illegitimate but that it is an easy prey for doubt, as later testing may show.

A CONTRACT AND A SIGNATURE

The good news of the Christian gospel is a covenant agreement, a contract that God offers to us. The gift of the Holy Spirit is the seal of his part of the contract; by committing ourselves to him we put our name to it too. It is not enough for us only to see the need of the contract (the essence of level one) or even the attractiveness and reliability of the terms (levels two and three). What is needed to make the contract binding and valid is our signature, a commitment of faith. Without this signature, however excellent the terms, the contract is only a piece of paper.

Personal knowledge always implies some degree of personal commitment to truth. Human thinking and language would dissolve into a topsy-turvy jumble of uncertainty if we were to use the word *know* as if it were interchangeable with words like *guess* or *dream*, or if we were to say *right* when we really meant *wrong*. The reason that knowing is different from guessing or dreaming is that knowledge implies an unspoken submission to what is real or thought to be real. I can legitimately say, "I know," and add in the same breath, "but I am open to being shown I am wrong." But if knowledge is to have any substantial meaning, I must never say, "I know," and then add, "but I am sure I am wrong."

If we say we know something, we are making a claim that contains a personal and responsible commitment to what we know. It is not that once we know something we commit ourselves to it, but that knowing something is itself a commitment. Knowledge is an acknowledgment of that which is believed to be true. Knowing is a response to something beyond us, so it is more than subjective. But it is also *our* response to something beyond us, so it is more than objective too. No one would die for a question mark, and no one can live on the basis of "maybe. . . ."

When you say, "I know this is true," you are really saying, "This is what I am convinced is the truth of the matter." What is true for all personal knowledge is also true for the knowledge assumed in faith. Hence, there is no true knowledge of God without personal conviction, and the idea of a healthy faith that has no personal commitment is a contradiction in terms. As G. K. Chesterton wrote of H. G. Wells, "He thought that the object of opening the mind is simply opening the mind. Whereas I am incurably convinced that the object of opening the mind, as of opening the mouth, is to shut it again on something solid."[1]

This means that, however objectively true something may or may not be, if I am not personally convinced of it, then for me personally it is not true. That is, objectively it may be true, but subjectively I refuse to accept it.

This shows the important difference between subjectivism in faith and subjectivism in doubt. The former says that because something is true for me it is necessarily true, while the latter says that because something is not true for me it is not true. Both notions are mistaken, but their respective dangers lead in opposite directions. Subjectivism in faith makes something out of nothing and turns fiction into fact. Subjectivism in doubt, on the other hand, turns something into nothing and makes fact into fiction.

BELIEVING THE TRUTH AS A LION KILLS

Notice again that doubt from lack of commitment has nothing whatever to do with the truth or falseness of a belief. The weakness is not in truth as the object of belief; the weakness is in the believer failing to enter into the obligations of believing. The problem is not that believers cannot genuinely believe *something*, but that they will not genuinely believe *anything*. If they appear to believe, it is only because their lack of conviction is covered by other supports for faith, such as the encouragement of fellow believers, so that the weakness is not exposed.

But take away the healthy assurance that grows from personal conviction and every pressure will bear down on the weakened commitment and raise tremors of uncertainty that grow into doubt. Without commitment, faith seems to cost more than we bargained for. Apart from conviction, each new voice of authority appears to have the same weight as the one we believe, and every moment of unreality calls in question the reality of all past experience. We are then inclined to think, "Perhaps our faith isn't true after all." But in all honesty we should reword that to "I never really believed it properly anyway." What is lacking is not the terms of the contract but the signature of the believer.

One common doorway to this doubt today is the celebrated "leap of faith" that completely bypasses the question of truth. People believe what they want to believe or need to believe, and that is that. They have no conviction of truth and no corresponding personal conviction in believing. So, not surprisingly, they are vulnerable to doubt. But when they doubt, it is they—not their belief—that has been weighed and found wanting.

Our Western weakness for "the leap of faith" is a bad case of this deficiency, but there are many milder ones. We need to revise all our notions of faith that see it as a weak form of assent and agreement. As a visiting Western Christian learned from an old Masai Christian:

> . . . [T]he word my Masai catechist, Paul, and I had used to convey *faith* was not a very satisfactory word in their language. It meant literally *"to agree to."* I, myself, knew the word had that shortcoming. He said "to believe" like that was similar to a white hunter shooting an animal with his gun from a great distance. Only his eyes and his fingers took part in the act. We should find another word.
>
> He said for a man really to believe is like a lion going after its prey. His nose and eyes and ears pick up the prey. His legs give him the speed to catch it. All the power in his body is involved in the terrible death leap and single blow to the neck with the front paw, the blow that actually kills. And as the animal goes down the lion envelops it in his arms (Africans refer to the front legs of an animal as its arms), pulls it to himself, and makes it part of himself. This is the way a lion kills. This is the way a man believes. This is what faith is.[2]

After all, the wise old African believer concluded:

> You told us of the High God, how we must search for him, even leave our land and our people to find him. But we have not done this. We have not left our land. We have not searched for him. He has searched for us. He has searched *us* out and found us. All the time we think we are the lion. In the end, the lion is God.[3]

RELATIVISM AND GROUP-THINK

Two features of today's world make this element of conviction all the more necessary. First, we face a climate of prevailing relativism, the unchallenged assumption of much modern thought. Relativism cuts the ground from under conviction and precipitates a crisis of authority. It sidesteps the basic question "Is it true?" and replaces it with "Does it work?" and "How does it feel?" The effect has been to reduce truth to timeliness, morality to usefulness, and personal faith to what feels good—for me.

Sometimes the loss of conviction works one way. Minds are unsettled, directions are changed and loyalties are switched, with a casual sense of conviction little better than impulse or fashion. At other times, loss of conviction works another way. Commitment is not based on conviction of truth but on personal need, so it is only for its own sake, but it becomes a form of passionate intensity, even fanaticism.

The combination encourages a dangerous tolerance of error and a specious humility toward truth. Since nothing is a matter of conviction of truth, everything can be taken with total seriousness or total lack of seriousness. G. K. Chesterton gave an early warning: "What we suffer from today is humility in the wrong place. Modesty has moved from the organ of ambition. Modesty has settled on the organ of conviction; where it was never meant to be. A man was meant to be doubtful about himself but undoubting about the truth. This has been exactly reversed."[4]

The modern tendency toward group thinking is a second feature that makes personal conviction more necessary than ever. For both good and bad reasons, the emphasis on individuality that has dominated the West since the close of the Middle Ages is now being discouraged in favor of emphasizing the wider group. Individuality is now viewed against wider frames of unity such as the tribe, the party, the race, the state, the balance of nature, the progress of evolution, and the historical process. The merits of individuality are being lumped together with the dangers, and both are being dismissed as "individualism." The advantages of unity over diversity, or collectivism over individualism, are assumed to be self-evident and the obvious collectivist overtones are ignored.

People in groups are now apt to think in ways that people in a more independently-minded age would have rejected. The obvious checks to this are a strong sense of individual identity, the courage to assume personal responsibility, a developed sense of right and wrong, and the ability to think for oneself. But these qualities have been so badly eroded that the controlling guards of critical thought are down. Large numbers of people are unthinkingly accepting what is sometimes harmless nonsense but could just as easily be fraudulent propaganda or dangerous lies.

Today's challenge to faith is gullibility, not credibility. The problem is not that it is too difficult to believe but that it is too easy. It is hard for people not to believe, for they slip in and out of belief spurred by a general will to believe and caressed by the gently shifting breezes of cultural fashion. Almost anything goes in the permissive climate, anything, that is, except those beliefs (like the Christian faith) that take truth and personal conviction seriously.

At first sight, overlooking truth has its advantages for the church. Thousands can turn or return to faith as part of the psychological and sociological undercurrents of our time. ("Yuppies come back to God to find values for their children.") But for every one who "goes with the flow" and discovers true faith, there are many who come to faith with the flow and go on from the faith with the flow. Without the anchor of personal conviction they are at the mercy of every ebb and flow of opinion. There is no iron in the new faith because it lacks conviction of truth and personal conviction.

THE KEY TO DISCIPLESHIP

Choice is one of the root ideas in the word *believe*, and this element of responsibility and commitment is the key to the "obedience of faith" that is the heart of Christian discipleship. Stress obedience apart from faith and you produce legalism. Stress faith apart from obedience and you produce cheap grace. For the person who becomes a Christian, the moment of comprehension leads to one conclusion only—commitment. The cost has been counted, a shoulder has been put to the yoke, a hand to the plow, and a contract for discipleship has been signed. The decision is irreversible. It is not faith going a second mile; it is faith making its first full step, and there is no going back.

The responsible commitment that is assumed in a small way in all personal knowledge comes into its own in the Christian faith. In the Christian faith, commitment is not only assumed, it is required. It is not only a premise of epistemology but a developed principle of theology. Faith is "obedience to the truth."[5] Discipleship is an undertaking that grows out of an understanding. What faith has seen, obedience is prepared to sign. This is the obedience of faith to which personal conviction leads.

Put differently, a conviction is nothing if it is not our own. Other things play their part in helping us to understand, but nothing can take its place. Unless each of us wrestles with the truth for ourselves, we will end up with opinions rather than convictions. Pascal warned that "hearsay is so far from being a criterion of belief that you should not believe anything until you have put yourself into the same state as if you had never heard it."[6] No conviction is truly our own unless we are prepared to hold it even if the rest of the world is against it. Athanasius *contra mundum* (against the world) is a stance we would not wish for ourselves but a stance that is implied in faith.

The note of conviction is prominent in biblical faith. "Choose here and now whom you will worship," Joshua challenged the people of Israel but did not pause for a reply: "But I and my family, we will worship the LORD."[7] "We have no need to answer you on this matter" is the calm response of Shadrach, Meshach, and Abednego to Nebuchadnezzar's threat. "If there is a god who is able to save us from the blazing furnace, it is our God whom we serve, and he will save us from your power, O king; but if not, be it known to your majesty that we will neither serve your god nor worship the golden image that you have set up."[8] "I know the one whom I have trusted," writes Paul from his prison cell, "and am confident of his power to keep safe what he has put into my charge until the great day."[9]

The same note is equally clear in the testimony of Christian history. Polycarp, the second-century Christian leader in Smyrna, faced a hostile mob and quietly refused to go back on his faith in Christ: "Eighty and six years have I served him, and he hath done me no wrong; how then can I blaspheme my King who saved me?"[10] Martin Luther, defending himself and his writings before the Holy Roman Emperor Charles V, closes his statement with the celebrated words: "My conscience is taken captive by God's word, I cannot and will not recant anything. On this I take my stand. I can do no other. So help me God."[11] The witness of history is as clear as it is stirring. And the examples we know are only the tip of the great, hidden iceberg of heroic faith that is Christian conviction through the centuries.

Not surprisingly, many opponents of the Christian faith have disliked this conviction. "Their pertinacity and inflexible obstinacy should certainly be punished," wrote the Younger Pliny to the Emperor Trajan, c. A.D. 112.[12] Others, like Alan Watts, have grudgingly admired it: "Without any disrespect it must be said that Christianity is pre-eminently the gamblers' religion. In no other religion are the stakes so high and the choice so momentous."[13] But both the ancient emperor and the modern mystic observe the same thing—the combination of conviction of truth and personal conviction is a hallmark of Christian discipleship. Without such commitment, there is no real faith.

IN MY OWN EXPERIENCE

Let me be personal here, for coming to grips with this point has been an important milestone in my own life as a Christian. I can see this now, yet it was not until nearly ten years after I came to faith in Christ that I finally faced the issue that whatever other influences had been involved in my conversion (such as my family and friends and the work of God in my life) there was a sense in which the decision to believe was fully my responsibility. I am not saying that my trusting God was "all up to me" but that I had to see that all of me was involved in trusting God. The decision to believe was one for which I at least was fully responsible.

Until then I had found that when difficulties came or doubts arose, I could always escape their force by not holding myself answerable for my own faith. This meant I could blame the problems on other people or on situations outside myself. The irresponsibility of this helped me to escape the force of the problems, but at the same time I was constantly troubled by suspicion. I had entered fully into the shared joys of Christian experience, but I had never quite gained the satisfaction that other Christians seemed to have. I was on the inside of Christian faith, yet in my mind I was also on the outside looking in. I was not prepared to commit myself completely in every situation, as I found myself as the actor and the spectator at the same time.

At times, in fact, there was a sense of hollowness about much of my faith. This came home to me when I was traveling alone in Southeast Asia for some months. I knew almost no one, and because of the language barrier I could speak freely with few people. The surrounding culture was fascinating but not my own. Slowly the pressures of its differences bore down on my thinking and decisions, prying open my defenses and forcing me to face questions I had not been conscious of before.

Why did I do things this way rather than that? How did I know that such-and-such a principle was right, especially when no one there shared it? How did I really know? And how had I chosen what was "right" and what was "wrong"? Were my beliefs my own or were they merely the product of my culture, my country, my education, or a legacy from my parents?

When I was separated from all these early influences, my choices became simple. For once in my life there was no need to believe as I did or act as I chose for any reasons other than that I was personally convinced it was right. Familiar people and influences were distant. They would never know or be affected. Existentially, they did not touch me at that moment. If I was to believe something or to choose to do something, the decision was one that I had to make *myself* and make *before God alone*.

It wasn't that I was doubting my faith or denying the reality of my becoming a Christian, but rather that, though I had genuinely believed ten years earlier, my commitment had been intertwined with the emotional comfort of sharing the beliefs and way of life of my family and certain friends. I had not only come to faith. I had also, as it were, "fallen in line" again, so that although I believed, my faith had been marked by a continuing lack of personal conviction.

I was convinced of it, but I was not staked on it. Partly I had believed for reasons that were beside the point, and I had used the emotional commitment I had found in this to cover for a lack of genuine commitment. I had been both committed and noncommittal. It was only after the resolution that this experience brought that I could say with a new reality, "This God is *my* God." The decisiveness and fresh conviction it brought made no difference to my theology and very little difference to my choices and values seen from the outside. The difference it made was internal. Now the choices and values are not only what I trust are right choices and correct beliefs; they are *my* choices, *my* beliefs, *my* convictions. Of course they are always more than my choice, but they are never less than my choice.

A CANCER OF UNREALITY

The type of doubt that is generated by a weak sense of personal conviction is not always immediately apparent. This doubt does not cry out in pain or groan in anguish. It has little intellectual sharpness, and its theology is often impeccable. It appears baffling because it seems to call no attention to itself. It is not rudely skeptical about the Christian faith, simply diffident about itself, and at first sight this looks appealing. Its defining feature is that it has none, except as time goes on, a growing sense of unreality.

Unreality is the heart of this doubt. People in this situation profess to believe the truth, but they have no serious engagement with truth. Without it, doubt is allowed to act like a cancer of unreality on faith. Or, to change the metaphor, a weak conviction acts on faith like a slipping clutch. The driver is experienced, the car is powerful, the engine is tuned, but the clutch will not engage. It can be the same with faith. A good mind and a warm heart can be made impotent if there is no commitment.

This sense of unreality marks only the opening stage of this doubt. It quickly leads to a second stage characterized chiefly by guilt. People in doubt know that their beliefs are true, but these beliefs are unreal to them. They grow ashamed of harboring doubts to which they know the answer themselves, but they keep the doubt to themselves, fugitive thoughts, locked away from the light of open discussion. This is doubt's incubation period, and the dark aura of guilty secrecy is an ideal womb. Finally doubt bursts out in a different form in its third stage of development.

Here doubt is most true to itself. Weak all along in terms of commitment, doubt now shows its colors and acts true to form by refusing to shoulder any responsibility for the unreality it has caused. It shifts the blame to belief. This is the moment when bad theology enters, not as a reason for doubt but as a rationale for the doubting that has already been going on. The doubt that was originally a result of an uncommitted belief becomes a rationale for committed unbelief. Through a clever about-turn, the doubter conceals his or her evasion of responsibility. Though their doubt is really an expression of not-being-committed, the doubter passes it off as an excuse for not-committing.

WHAT STAGE HAS IT REACHED?

The remedy for this doubt begins with checking which stage the doubt has reached and what is the root of the lack of conviction. Only when the cause of the doubt has been understood and dealt with can faith be reengaged and personal conviction encouraged.

There are many reasons why people have a diminished sense of personal conviction and some are easy to deal with. Many Christians, for example, have "grown into faith" almost imperceptibly (through, say, their family) so they have never become aware of the need for their own convictions. This is a common feature of faith in countries where there is an established or state church—faith is almost inherited. Others have come to faith at a particular moment in their lives, and know it, but have believed for good reasons mixed in with less good reasons, so that their faith was never based on a strong, true conviction.

With these people the remedy lies in pointing out the responsibility that faith requires. Usually, their problem is not that they could not take on this responsibility before but that they were not asked to. There might be some question now as to whether they will, but there is no question that they can if they want to.

But there are still others who have no sense of conviction because of problems on a far deeper level, such as a crisis of identity. It takes someone to know something. If conviction in belief is like the authorizing signature on a contract or a check, then people who have no sense of themselves will have no "name" to sign to what they believe. The contract may be good or the check generous, but it lacks the binding authorization of a signature.

Imagine a millionaire who has decided to donate to a charity. He writes out a generous check and sends it off. Later he has second thoughts. He gets cold feet and phones his bank manager asking him to stop the check. But then, just as he is halfway through explaining it, the secretary of the charity organization is shown in, wreathed in smiles and eager to thank him for his generosity. So he is caught between the two of them, embarrassed to welcome his guest and unable to say more on the phone.

There are doubters who are like this. Their weakness is not that they will not commit themselves to God but that they do not commit themselves to anything. Nothing terrifies them more than the responsibility of choosing. They do anything to avoid choosing, and if events force them to make a choice, they question it by raking over the ashes of the decision until it is dead and cold. Even when they make the right choice, they don't let the choice go through. They write out a check, but it never gets cashed because it's taken back at once, and they are paralyzed and embarrassed by the dilemmas they create for themselves. As a Spanish proverb puts it, "Among the safest of courses, the safest of all is to doubt."

The remedy for these people is to see where the problem lies—with them, not with God. It isn't that God is unreal; lack of commitment has made everything unreal. The shadow is not over God; it is over anything else. What they must do is relearn to choose and commit themselves to the consequences of their choice. As they do this, trusting in God's help, inching forward like a baby taking its first steps, a sense of reality will return to their faith as well as their lives. The early choices will be painful, of course, but in much the same way that "pins and needles" are painful when your leg has gone to sleep. Pins and needles can even hurt so much that we would almost prefer to let the leg sleep on. But not really. Better pins and needles than no leg at all.

AS NOW, SO THEN

This type of doubt is already aggravated by the contemporary crisis of identity. It may grow even worse if there is a further hardening of society's attitudes toward the Christian faith. It takes conviction to stand firm when there is a price to pay, when a strong authority is openly hostile, or when the surrounding consensus considers belief ridiculous, harmful, or unpatriotic. This is already the position of many Christians in the world today, and those of us with more freedom now may well experience it before the end of this century. If this is the case, Christians most likely to buckle under the heat will be those who lack personal conviction. The difference between an enduring faith and a nominal faith is largely at this point.

It is none too soon to be aware of the challenges we may face, but our security does not lie in our brilliant forecasting of where we may be tested. That was Peter's mistake at the arrest of Jesus and why his bravado collapsed into betrayal—he was ready to die for Jesus but not to speak up for him. For one thing, it is for the Holy Spirit to tell us what we are to say in that hour. For another thing, the people we prove to be in that hour will be determined, not by our thinking about that hour, but by our thinking and living in this hour. We will measure up to tomorrow's requirements only by measuring up to today's. Fifteen minutes in the limelight may make us a celebrity, but character is built in the unseen succession of little obediences and little acts of faith.

"As now, so then" applies also to conviction. We need to examine ourselves honestly to see whether our convictions are truly our own or merely inherited beliefs or shared opinions. It is not that God is testing us to see whether we believe or not. God does not need to find out whether we will stand or fall. He knows that already. It is we who do not know, and like Peter, we can be too sure of ourselves for our own good.

As C. S. Lewis warned,

> Your bid will not be serious if nothing much is staked on it. And you will never discover how serious it was until the stakes are raised horribly high; until you find that you are playing not for counters or sixpences but for every penny you have in the world. Nothing less will shake a man—or at any rate a man like me—out of his merely verbal thinking and his merely notional beliefs. He has to be knocked silly before he comes to his senses. Only torture will bring out the truth.[14]

C. S. Lewis was writing after the death of his wife, but his words apply equally to the lesser crises of faith we all face today.

As the Apostle John was told by the Third Angel who described
the pressure of crises on faith, "This is where the fortitude of
God's people has its place—in keeping God's commands and
remaining loyal to Jesus."[15]Martin Luther, whose own convictions had been tempered and proved like the finest steel, knew
well that in the hour of trial each person must have his or her
own convictions, or he will find himself with none. His warning should put the importance of conviction in faith beyond
all question: "Bear in mind, then, that when you face death or
persecution, I cannot be with you, or you with me. Every man
must then fight for himself."[16]

———◼—————

CHAPTER 7

NO SIGN
OF LIFE

Doubt from
Lack of Growth

Sometimes it is easy to be so taken up with learning to start something that the question of what comes next never crosses our minds. I remember feeling like this learning to ski in Switzerland. Like everyone else, I was concentrating desperately on standing up and staying up. But suddenly, after all the effort, I was off. And that's when it hit me. What do I do next? How do I keep going? How do I stop? In our desire to get started in something we often forget that starting is not an end in itself. We are getting started to go somewhere or to do something.

Becoming a Christian can be the same. It is easy to forget that becoming a Christian is only the beginning. The journey of a thousand miles begins with the first step, but the purpose of the first step is the whole journey. It is not the other way round.

The first four varieties of doubt stem from a deficiency of understanding in coming to faith in Christ. They are all common but unnecessary in the sense that, if we enter into the full biblical understanding of faith, there is no need for any of these doubts to grow. We can go on in the Christian life with confidence, even at these potentially dangerous points. But these are not the end of possible doubts for the believer. They are only the end of doubts at faith's beginning. We must now examine some of the other varieties of doubt that Christians face as they go on in their new life.

The fifth doubt enters right there—when Christians do *not* go on, when they do not grow, when they fail to experience and express their new life, when they simply fail to practice the truth. This is the doubt we will examine in this chapter, and again our goal is to see how it grows from a deficiency of faith and how this can be remedied. What moves, grows, and bears fruit shows life. What is inert or barren may be dead. This does not mean, of course, that everything that is not growing, moving, or bearing fruit is dead. But it does mean there may be *no way to tell* if it is alive or not. Movement, growth, and fruit are unmistakable signs of life.

The Christian life is new life, the life of Jesus Christ implanted in us as Christian believers, transforming us and bearing fruit through him. Like all life this life is nothing if it is not lived out. Christian thinking, Christian choices, Christian action do not bring life into Christians. They are expressions of life that is already there. Without this prior life, our faith is barren, mechanical, and dead.

So a special challenge to faith comes here: If faith is not being practiced, how is anyone to know it is real? If there are no signs of growth or fruit, how are we to know it is alive? If we are unable to answer these questions, it does not necessarily mean that there is no life but that, at the moment, there is no way to tell. This is what opens the door to doubt.

Putting it like this can be very unhelpful, for it may suggest the misleading picture of the Christian life as a plant that periodically must be pulled up by the roots to see whether it is growing. That is not only bad for the plant, it is impossible for the Christian.

We must find a more helpful angle from which to examine growth and fruitfulness as a test for signs of life. One possibility is to think in terms of worldviews. Just as a plant grows or withers, so a worldview must be developed and practiced and produce results or it will be discarded as impractical. Of course, being a Christian means much more than just having and using a particular worldview. But to examine faith's growth from this viewpoint is extremely useful in understanding this doubt.

A WORLDVIEW IN PRACTICE

The test of faith around which this doubt centers is not as dramatic as it is with other doubts. Each of us has his or her own worldview, but few people are consciously aware of it and this is as it should be. What health is to the body, a working philosophy is to the mind. The mind may be at its healthiest when its owner is least aware of his or her worldview.

But even when people are unconscious of their philosophies of life, they are not uncritical of them. Throughout their lives, down below the surface of their conscious thoughts, emotions, and choices, they are constantly testing and trying out their worldviews. For a worldview, the process of living is a nonstop examination by experience in which only the practicable is preserved.

Human beings are meaning-mongers. We are driven by a deep desire for meaning and belonging. We can live meaningfully only if we can make sense of our situation and through that find security in our world. Part of being human is the need to find a framework through which life can be interpreted, so that the bare facts and raw experiences of life are given coherence and meaning. All our views and values are a close-knit series of beliefs that are rooted at bottom in our basic assumptions. Deeper even than a value system there lies in each of our minds a meaning system. Thus our judgments, our decisions, our principles, and our opinions are not arbitrary or unconnected but have a hidden logic and interdependence that is rooted in our basic worldview and presuppositions.

The usefulness of a person's worldview depends on how well it can order and handle experience for him or her. Once people make a worldview their own by believing it, it will either be proved in practice or disproved by being impracticable. At this level, what they believe either works or it is useless—nice-sounding theory is irrelevant. Here faith is not what people say they believe but what they show they believe. Their faith is what they function on. It has nothing to do with profession, everything to do with practice.

The reality test for faith at this level is life. Every moment and each new experience challenge faith for an interpretation. Can faith order the new experience, cope with it, handle it, assimilate it? Or will the new experience undermine faith, proving too much for it to understand and assimilate? If faith is to continue supplying a person's worldview, it must answer this challenge constantly and completely. Equally its answer must be practical, not theoretical, and it must be fresh and contemporary, not yesterday's answer to today's challenge. Either faith will rise to the occasion, and if so, it will grow in the process. Or else it will fall and retreat, losing authority, imperceptibly growing weaker, and to that extent, becoming unreal.

Doubt waits in the wings at this point of moment-by-moment challenge. If faith plays its part, faith grows stronger and more assured, dominating the stage so that doubt can make no entry. But if faith hesitates only slightly or shows the slightest sign of retreat, doubt takes its cue and slips on stage. A part of life, an area of experience has proved too much for faith to handle, and this unmanaged situation calls in question faith's authority and makes room for doubt. The process is not one of which we are aware, of course, but it is no less dangerous for being unconscious. The doubt generated begins as a tiny crack in faith's authority, and it may take a while before it widens. But left unchecked it will only be a matter of time before it breaks through into the conscious mind.

All human beings have a worldview, so this testing of faith is common to all and not just Christians. The difference for us as Christians is that our worldview operates on a conscious as well as an unconscious level, and therefore we become sensitive to unreality much sooner. We are not unique in this. Rather, like the worldviews of Hindus or humanists, our worldview can be developed explicitly and formally and not just left at implicit and informal levels.

If we view growth in terms of putting a worldview to work, we can see that there is nothing mysterious about the loss of growth and vitality that leads to this type of doubt. It has nothing to do with God's displeasure or any projected sense of abandonment or supposed spiritual withdrawal. Doubt arises naturally because truth that is unpracticed will soon be taken to be impracticable. And, since practicability is an absolute essential for a worldview, truth that is impracticable will soon be discarded as untrue. It is not that the Christian faith is true because it works, but if it is not put to work, a severe doubt is cast over its truthfulness.

LITTLE BY LITTLE AND CHOICE BY CHOICE

The key to this kind of doubt is simple: People do not so much lose their faith as cease to use their faith. This doubt is characterized by standing still, by indecision and drift. The French novel-

ist, Georges Bernanos, describes this in the words of a young
country priest writing in his private journal:

> No. I have not lost my faith. The expression "to lose one's
> faith," as one might a purse or a ring of keys has always
> seemed to me rather foolish. It must be one of those sayings
> of bourgeois piety, a legacy of those wretched priests of the
> eighteenth century who talked so much.
>
> Faith is not a thing which one "loses," we merely cease
> to shape our lives by it. That is why old-fashioned confes-
> sors are not far wrong in showing a certain amount of scep-
> ticism when dealing with "intellectual crises," doubtless far
> more rare than people imagine. An educated man may come
> by degrees to tuck away his faith in some back corner of his
> brain, where he can find it again on reflection, by an effort
> of memory: yet even if he feels a tender regret for what no
> longer exists and might have been, the term "faith" would
> nevertheless be inapplicable to such an abstraction.[1]

This type of doubt is very courteous. One might almost say
that it is a very civilized way of doubting, as if a slow choice to
disbelieve was no choice at all. Personal responsibility is side-
stepped so that faith can eventually be laid aside with a kind of
courteous and chivalrous regret. The manner is deceiving, but,
stripped to its essentials, the complaint against faith is blunt:
Faith does not work; it must be discarded.

The question the doubter does not ask is whether faith was
really useless or simply not used. What would you think of a boy
who gave up learning to ride a bicycle, complaining that he hurt
himself because his bicycle stopped moving so he had no choice
but to fall off? If he wanted to sit comfortably while remaining stationary, he should not have chosen a bicycle but a chair.
Similarly faith must be put to use, or it will become useless.

Charles Darwin gives us a celebrated description of such a

slow erosion of faith in his autobiography: "I gradually came to disbelieve in Christianity as a divine revelation. . . . Disbelief crept over me at a very slow rate, but was at last complete. The rate was so slow that I felt no distress, and have never since doubted even for a single second that my conclusion was correct."[2]

This is the way that many people doubt, little by little, choice by choice, thought by thought. Faith is not torn up, it is merely frayed. It is not eaten away suddenly but nibbled at the corners. It is not hit by a bolt of lightning, it is the victim of the slow erosion of many winters. In a time of cultural and religious decline like our own, the incidence of this doubt is more common than ever. As C. S. Lewis observed, "If you examined a hundred people who had lost their faith in Christianity, I wonder how many of them would turn out to have been reasoned out of it by honest argument? Do not most people simply drift away?"[3]

Lewis even recognized this doubt in himself. He once wrote his great friend Arthur Greeves,

> The trouble with me is *lack of faith*. I have no *rational* ground for going back on the arguments that convinced me of God's existence: but the irrational deadweight of my old sceptical habits, and the spirit of this age, and the cares of the day, steal away all my lively feeling of the truth, and often when I pray I wonder if I am not posting letters to a non-existent address. Mind you I don't *think* so—the whole of my reasonable mind is convinced: but I often *feel* so.[4]

We have a graphic biblical example of this in the state of the late first century church in Sardis, in Asia Minor, to which Jesus wrote: "Though you have a name for being alive, you are dead. Wake up, and put some strength into what is left, which must otherwise die!"[5] Under the penetrating gaze of Christ the difference between the actual and the apparent, the reality and the reputation, was all too obvious. He knew that the seeming peace was a sleep that would end in death.

In a curious way, the state of the church in Sardis mirrored the celebrated history of the great city it was in. Built by the fabled Croesus in the sixth century B.C., the citadel of Sardis had been constructed on a promontory of rock and was regarded as impregnable. But twice in its long history the citadel had fallen, not because of the force of strategy of superior armies but simply because the garrison had been so overconfident that there had been no vigilance. It had therefore been caught off guard with its defenses unmanned. Spiritually speaking, the Sardis Church was in the same danger. Self-confident in the reputation they enjoyed, they were careless about putting their faith to work, and the drift toward death was well under way.

A living faith is a relationship, and, like any relationship, it must be cherished, nurtured, fostered, and prized for itself. Think of any special friendship you enjoy. Was it all there when you first met each other? Or is its richness many-splendored, a mosaic of all the moments of shared experience?

Like an art or a skill, faith must not only be learned but kept in practice and developed. Just as a concert pianist practices for eight hours a day or a marathon runner covers fifteen, twenty, or thirty miles in road training, so faith grows strong in believing but atrophies if out of use. Nothing is more pathetic than the sight of a Christian of forty or fifty attempting to get by on the faith he had when he was twenty, especially since the intervening years have seen development and maturity in every other area. Such faith is little more than a memory.

PUTTING FAITH TO THE TEST

What is the antidote to this variety of doubt? To put faith to work. To stretch it, to put it on the line, to prove it in the crucible of experience, and so to let it deepen and grow with the testing of life. This doubt is not in need of comfort but challenge. The problem is not that faith is untrue but that it is untried. As Martin Luther pointed out, "The true, living faith, which the Holy Spirit instills into the heart, simply cannot be idle."[6] Or as George Whitefield, the great eighteenth-century preacher whose life was a blazing torch in God's hand, wrote in his diary, "I am never better than when I am on the full stretch for God."[7]

We all face this challenge. Faith must go on being exercised. Faith must mean everything today or in some tomorrow it may mean nothing. Yesterday's experiences, insights, answers to prayer, ways of putting things were completely legitimate and satisfying yesterday, but today is another day. God's truth and God's love will always be fresh, but will the same be said of our response? Will our faith and our love for him be as fresh? Paul's question to the Christians in Corinth is a question for us all: "Examine yourselves: are you living the life of faith? Put yourselves to the test."[8]

Doubt from an unused faith is widespread. We could point to several factors to explain it. The continuation of state churches in post-Christian cultures, the equation of Christian values and cultural norms, the presence of Christian ghettos and the insulated pipeline of Christian education, the concentration on faith in conversion rather than faith in living, the preoccupation with evangelism at the expense of ethics—these are all features of faith today that discourage faith from being stretched and applied. And therefore foster doubt.

KEEP FAITH FIT

Like an athlete in training, faith must keep itself fit. It must be trim and in good shape. It must keep its hand in and never be out of practice. It will have its limits, but it will know them and do its best to extend them. What faith fears above all is the test that shows that its training has gone to seed, its muscles have grown soft, its confidence has been misplaced. In short, faith will exercise.

Not surprisingly, many of the biblical pictures of faith are strenuous, active, and energetic. Faith is the athlete straining for the finishing line, the boxer kept in superb condition by his training, the soldier stripped to his essential equipment.[9] There is no place for the poorly trained runner, the overweight boxer moving sluggishly round the ring, the reluctant soldier distracted by civilian pursuits and preoccupations. Faith presses forward or is pushed back. Faith trains or grows slack.

Bunyan depicted the danger of inaction in his charming but vacuous character, Mr. Talkative, whose companionship was so beguiling to Christian and Faithful. Faithful was the first to remember something of his reputation. "I have heard of you that you are a man whose religion lies in talk, and that your conversation [way of life] gives this your mouth-profession the lie."[10] But Christian sees through Mr. Talkative too and warns his friend,

> He thinks that learning and saying will make a good Christian and thus he deceiveth his own soul. Hearing is but as the sowing of the seed; talking is not sufficient to prove that the fruit is indeed in the heart and life and let us assure ourselves, that at the day of doom, men shall be judged according to their fruits. It will not be said then, "Did you believe?" but "Were you doers or talkers only?," and accordingly shall they be judged. The end of the world is compared to our harvest, and you know men at harvest regard nothing but fruit.[11]

Bunyan's character is not so much one type of believer as a part of every believer. He may well be the nominal Christian who sits near us in church, but he is certainly the other person in our hearts. It is to the Mr. Talkative in us all that Jesus often addressed his sternest warnings. The Sermon on the Mount closes with unrelenting severity, directing warning upon warning against an empty profession of faith, making it clear beyond question that the only faith that counts is faith that obeys.

> A good tree cannot bear bad fruit, or a poor tree good fruit. And when a tree does not yield good fruit it is cut down and burnt. That is why I say you will recognize them by their fruits.
>
> Not everyone who calls me "LORD, LORD" will enter the kingdom of Heaven, but only those who do the will of my heavenly Father. . . .
>
> What then of the man who hears these words of mine and acts upon them? He is like a man who had the sense to build his house on rock. . . . But what of the man who hears these words of mine and does not act upon them? He is like a man who was foolish enough to build his house on sand.[12]

In an incident in Mark's Gospel Jesus asks the question: "'Who is my mother? Who are my brothers?' And looking round at those who were sitting in the circle about him he said, 'Here are my mother and my brothers. Whoever does the will of God is my brother, my sister, my mother.'"[13] The practice of truth and the obedience of faith could easily be construed merely as external marks of discipleship. But Jesus restores them to their proper place at the heart of faith. Each at its highest is a part of the intimate family relationship that is the fellowship of faith. For faith to obey is for faith to come into its own. For faith to practice the truth is for faith to be most itself. Obedience is the blood-tie of the new community. This is the style of faith that makes life a rich experience and effectively rules out the possibility of this doubt.

CHAPTER 8

COUP D'ÉTAT
FROM WITHIN

Doubt from
Unruly Emotions

I know someone who is afraid of flying. Several times I have heard well-meaning people try to persuade her that it is much safer to fly in an airplane than to drive in a car. Perhaps one day someone might convince her, either by marshaling an impressive array of statistics and well-documented evidence or by appealing to factors that are essentially emotional, if not manipulative. Their case might be convincing, even irrefutable. But I know she would still prefer to drive in a car.

The strength of the rational argument would be no match for the power of the emotions. It's one thing to think rationally in an airport lounge and another thing to feel rational on the runway. But when the seat belts are fastened and the engines are revving, the voice of reason can hardly be heard above the roar of the emotions. The problem is not that reason attacks faith but that the emotions overwhelm reason as well as faith, and it is impossible for reason to dissuade them.

The sixth variety of doubt comes just at the point where

the believer's emotions (vivid imagination, changing moods, erratic feelings, intense reactions) rise up and overpower the understanding of faith. Out-voted, out-gunned, faith is pressed back and hemmed in by the unruly mob of raging emotions that only a while earlier were quiet, orderly citizens of the personality. Reason is cut down, obedience is thrown out, and for a while the rule of the emotions is as sovereign as it is violent. The coup d'état is complete.

Put differently, it is silly to assume that if we accept something as true, we will go on regarding it as true until some other reason turns up and undermines the original belief. The human mind is ruled by emotions as well as reason, and the emotions are often stronger. C. S. Lewis wrote, "unless you teach your moods 'where they get off,' you can never be a sound Christian or even a sound atheist, but just a creature dithering to and fro, with its beliefs really dependent on the weather and the state of its digestion."[1]

THE PLACE OF THE EMOTIONS

The basic issue of faith is the question of credibility. Is what I believe true? Is the person whom I trust trustworthy? Coming to faith is a question of grappling with the truth of the matter and the trustworthiness of the person. Is there compelling evidence or not?

Subjective elements play their part in the decision to believe. But if faith is not to be make-believe, objective considerations must finally determine whether faith is true or misplaced. Understanding and choice are both essential to genuine belief, and they are always more important than the emotions in conversion.

Needless to say, conversion may be profoundly emotional because it is a complete change involving the whole person. But however emotional it is, the emotions alone do not effect conversion. This is not because the Christian faith is unemotional but because this is how human knowing works anyway. The Christian faith, in fact, has a very high place for the emotions, but in coming to believe the place for understanding and choosing truth is primary and the place for the emotions is secondary.

This statement is fine in theory. But even if we come to faith with our emotions playing their proper part, it is quite another thing to keep that balance in continuing to believe. And, of course, not all of us started with it anyway. Perhaps the greatest single human factor in explaining why faith does not go on as it began is the explosive power of the emotions subsequent to conversion.

If we were not marked by the results of the Fall, we would experience an unconscious natural harmony between our understanding, willing, and feeling. All our actions and reactions would be whole. But none of us enjoy that perfect balance now, and the alienation of sin means that we are alienated not only from God and each other but also from ourselves. The deep harmony within each of us has been lost. For some people, the alienation is so extreme that it leads to severe emotional disorder. But for most of us the hassle of living with our contradictory "selves" and struggling with our conflicting emotions is a run-of-the-mill aspect of living. We are so used to putting up with the brokenness of our fallen human nature that we tend to accept it as normal and take it for granted.

The alienation of sin plays equal havoc in our understanding, our choosing, and our feeling. It is not that one of them has "fallen further" than the other two. But the emotions are distinctive for one important reason. They are that part of us most vulnerable to outside influences, and in this sense, they are the part of us most easily manipulated. For some people even the body is less immune to sickness than the emotions are to "catching" whatever is around. Our understanding can be persuaded not to believe, and our conviction can be broken. But when we are under pressure our emotions tend to throw in the towel long before our understanding or our will.

This gives the impression that the emotions are a problem because they are weak. But it is just the reverse: The real problem is that they are too strong. Not only are our emotions easily influenced; they are highly influential. Once persuaded, they become the powerful persuaders, and here is their danger.

The emotions and the imagination may sometimes be under the control of reason and understanding, but they are seldom tamed for long. Just as often the emotions rise up against reason in their own special kind of "palace coup" within the personality. Then they carry everything before them in a flood of feeling that overwhelms logic and reason. At such times the frailty of rationality is all too apparent. Gossamer thin, featherlight, glass-brittle, reason seems to stand no chance against the elemental power of fear, anger, hatred, jealousy, desire, or whatever is moving us. We then become little better than the "two silly women" about whom George Macdonald wrote:

> They had a feeling, or a feeling had them, till another feeling came and took its place. When a feeling was there, they felt as if it would never go; when it was gone, they felt as if it had never been; when it returned, they felt as if it had never gone.[2]

Because we human beings are so volatile we need to be realistic. Thomas à Kempis wrote, "It is good counsel, that when fervor of spirit is kindled within thee, thou shouldst consider how it will be, when that light shall leave thee." After all, he added, "If great saints were so dealt with, we that are weak and poor ought not to despair, if we be sometimes hurt and sometimes cold...."[3]

ELIJAH AND THE KINGDOM OF DESPAIR

This sixth doubt is another that has nothing specifically to do with the Christian faith. The situation is not that Christians have emotional doubts while all other people enjoy certainty. Everyone has emotional doubts and, naturally, we Christians experience ours in the context of our Christian faith.

A defining feature of this emotional uncertainty is that it has little to do with the content of belief and everything to do with the believer. Pascal wryly noted, "Put the world's greatest philosopher on a plank that is wider than need be: if there is a precipice below, although his reason may convince him that he is safe, his imagination will prevail."[4] James Thurber made the same point: "Every man is occasionally visited by the suspicion that the planet on which he is riding is not really going anywhere. These black doubts creep up on a man just before thunderstorms, or at six in the morning when the steam begins to knock solemnly in the pipes, or during his confused wanderings in the forest beyond Euphoria after a long night of drinking."[5]

The classic biblical example is the deep depression and suicidal longings of Elijah, the ninth-century B.C. prophet in Israel. "He came upon a broom-bush, and sat down under it and prayed for death: 'It is enough,' he said; 'now, LORD, take my life, for I am no better than my fathers before me.'"[6] Viewed from one angle this despairing collapse of will and indulgent self-pity seem incomprehensible. Here is Elijah at the high point of his ministry, recognized, vindicated, successful. Everything seems to be his for the taking. The crowds were behind him, the royal power was humbled, his enemies were largely wiped out, his cause was vindicated, and then suddenly at the threat from one woman—Jezebel—his courage crumples, and he runs for his life. Nothing appears more unreasonable.

But looked at from another angle, it is highly understandable. Elijah has snapped under the strain of the emotional intensity. The grueling demands of public confrontation have summoned up and exhausted his reserves of strength. The lonely years in the desert followed by the dramatic road race to Jezreel have so stretched his emotions that at a single threat he folds. It is not God who had let him down but his emotions that had overpowered his faith and reason, and plunged him into a trough of despair. Writing of a harrowing period in his ministry in the seventh century B.C., the prophet Jeremiah expressed the same emotion. Physically drained and emotionally exhausted, his faith had weakened too: "Then I cry out that my strength has gone and so has my hope in the LORD."[7]

However firm our understanding in faith and however strong our wills, there is no absolute guarantee against doubt making inroads into faith through our emotions. Exhaustion, loneliness, a long drawn out illness, an accident, bereavement, overwhelming tiredness, a flash of anger or jealousy, or even being undernourished—any of these give the emotions opportunity to usher in doubt. Battered emotions can produce a crop of doubts just as devastating as the militant atheist's toughest questions. Oswald Chambers wisely advises: "in taking an estimate of yourself, always take into account the capacity for depression."[8]

Martin Luther, a man of deep emotions, was very realistic at this point. "Eve got into trouble," he wrote, "when she walked in the garden alone. I have my worst temptations when I am by myself."[9] C. S. Lewis admitted similarly that he never had doubts except in a hotel room—alone and away from home. Earlier, Augustine disliked traveling and the winter season so much that he used them as a metaphor for life on earth in a fallen world.

REFUGE WITH CHRIST
AMONG CHRIST'S ENEMIES

Since emotionally rooted doubts are fired by the imagination, they make up in color and drama what they lack in logic. The facts of the matter are the same, but when the imagination speaks, it magically creates its own reality, and a different perspective is put on everything. What was real before is only a shadow now. What was nothing before has become everything.

As John Bunyan's Christian and Hopeful languished in the dungeons of Doubting Castle, a dark night of distress settled over Christian, and he forgot the certainties, joys, and triumphs of his pilgrimage up to that point. Hopeful prods him to recall the past: "Rememberest thou not how valiant thou has been heretofore; Apollyon could not crush thee, nor could all that thou did hear, or feel, or see in the Valley of the Shadow of Death; what hardship, terror, and amazement has thou already gone through, and art thou now nothing but fear?"[10]

The entry point for such a doubt need not be a lofty problem. Some little pinprick discomfort is far more effective—for example, an issue completely removed from God and theology, perhaps just an opinion of a fellow Christian. Granted even the strongest faith, doubt can usually be guaranteed a good run here. God's truth is as unshakable as before, faith is as firm in its convictions, but with the sudden fleeting thought of a Christian who is even the slightest bit ridiculous, distasteful, or different, the clear certainty of faith can become strangely muddied by emotions of embarrassment, hostility, or superiority.

Does anything match the frustration we can feel with our fellow believers? No doubt the problem is partly a projection of the frustration we feel with ourselves, and it probably means that others have the same problem with us. But one moment the sheer diversity of Christians seems a many-splendored thing of joy and wonder, while the next moment the same diversity is all individualism, oddness, and peculiarity. It isn't our theology that has changed, only our emotions.

But the occasion may be far more than a pinprick of discomfort or frustration. For example, when the problem is not frustration but pain caused by our fellow-believers, it can itself become a cause of doubt. Peter Abelard, the twelfth-century Sorbonne theologian, was the lifetime butt of envy and slander. Bitterly, he once wrote to a friend, he never heard that an assembly of ecclesiastics had met without thinking it was convened to condemn him. "Often, God knows, I fell into such a state of despair that I thought of quitting the realm of Christendom and going over to the heathen, there to live a quiet Christian life among the enemies of Christ at the cost of what tribute was asked."[11]

Abelard never followed his proposed solution—"taking refuge with Christ among Christ's enemies."[12] But, like Abelard and Job before him, anyone who has suffered the vicious attacks of fellow Christians knows the temptation of this doubt. But we must remember too its emotional base. God remains true though his people are sometimes treacherous. Our emotions are devastated, but our faith and God's faithfulness have not changed.

Pascal, musing on the weakness of reason before the emotions, concluded: "It is the same with knowledge, for illness removes it."[13] Later, in a similar vein, he spoke of how imagination can toy with reason: "Reason may object in vain, it cannot fix the price of things."[14]

C. S. Lewis made the same point in a helpful warning for newly converted Christians.

Supposing a man's reason once decides that the weight of evidence is for it. I can tell that man what is going to happen to him in the next few weeks. There will come a moment when there is bad news, or he is in trouble or is living among a lot of other people who do not believe it, and all at once his emotions will rise up and carry out a sort of blitz on his belief. Now faith, in the sense of which I am using the word, is the art of holding onto things your reason has once accepted, in spite of our change of moods.[15]

HEART AND MIND

There are several reasons why emotionally grounded doubt is common. Some are natural. For example, many people come to faith as teenagers or students, a time when all our decisive experiences have a strong emotional component; such as leaving home or falling in love.

Other reasons are more troublesome. For example, Americans have a characteristic American heresy—in the various forms of positive thinking, faith-in-faith replaces faith in God. To which Oswald Chambers has a sharp rejoinder, "Be ruthless with yourself if you are given to talking about the experiences you have had. Faith that is sure of itself is not faith. Faith that is sure of God is the only faith there is."[16]

Some reasons are inexcusable. For example, many Western Christians put an emphasis on emotions that is exaggerated and unbalanced by biblical standards. Often they discount the place of the understanding, too, and they justify the pride of place given to the emotions by appealing to a correct-sounding division between "head" and "heart."

Certainly God constantly speaks in the Bible to the human

heart. But the biblical understanding of *heart* and our modern understanding of *heart* are not the same. The Bible's understanding is almost the opposite of modern usage. In the Bible, *heart* can be translated as emotions in only a fraction of its many hundreds of uses. In the overwhelming majority of cases, it makes nonsense of the passage to translate it this way. Understood biblically, *heart* refers to the seat of the whole human person, the true self. In most cases, it refers to our understanding and not our emotions.

Mistaken teaching spawns a view of faith that is unbiblical, weak, and ineffective in combating doubts that come from an emotional source. The battle is lost before it begins. The understanding was not in control in time of faith, so it is too much to expect it to be in control in time of doubt. The emotions were everything when faith was there, and now that doubt is there they are still everything. All that is different is that they have changed sides.

But if the emotions are really all that matters, then neither faith nor doubt have anything to do with truth; they are simply the names that the emotions give to their changing moods.

STRANGERS IN A STRANGE LAND

Another reason this doubt is common today is the effect of social isolation on many Christians. This is less true of Christians in the West, although we too are in a curious situation in a society that is increasingly pluralistic in private life and secular in public life. Pluralism makes for freedom in some ways, but always within heavy constraints—we are most free in private, for example, but even private freedom is shaped by powerful forces such as consumerism, mass media, and shared ideas of tolerance. In a mass society, the effect is to create a shared world of reference, corralling society into subtle general attitudes with the whip of the constantly repeated word and message (the power of the shared joke, the shared value system, the shared ideology). Diversity is encouraged but only within definite, if unmentioned, limits, and tolerance itself can be highly selective. There is no official pecking order of philosophies and beliefs, let alone a party line. But an unofficial one is strong. The latest and most novel ideas are usually at the top of the ladder, and what is thought of as "yesterday's way of thinking" defines the bottom rung. Today's scarlet letter is not A for adultery but I for incorrect.

Being a Christian in such a society means swimming upstream. Ignorance of the Christian faith, not to speak of prejudice and caricature, is as common as understanding. The courage of one's convictions must be a fact to the Christian and not a figure of speech. A certain inescapable loneliness is felt in this situation that tends to demoralize the emotions.

Think of a freshman in a philosophy class where the case against the Christian faith is a continuing trial by scorn. Imagine a Christian professor of anthropology, misunderstood by her fellow believers as much as by her secular colleagues ("How could a Christian be in that field?"). Put yourself into some of the situations that believers daily face alone—the army canteen, the factory floor, the hospital ward, the business office. You don't have to imagine a situation particularly difficult, hostile, or "pagan." That might almost be easier. What is hard for believers is the constant burden of being different, of being the "odd person out," or of living in two worlds at once. The pressure of such loneliness can lead to doubt.

These pressures are even worse in countries that are hostile to the Christian faith. Before the collapse of Marxism a close friend wrote to me from Poland. Teaching as a professor in a Marxist university, he found that the Christian groups were retreating from the world, rigid in their ways of thinking. They are groups, as he put it, "with whom I will never have a common language. So I am pretty alone with the religious struggling that still goes on in me, and I very much feel like giving up."

My friend's loneliness was made more painful by the fact that he is a sensitive, Christian thinker, and the agonized doubts he went on to raise were inspired by isolation as much as by purely intellectual dilemmas. In replying, I could have entered into long philosophical and theological discussions, but I sensed that what was wanted to silence those doubts was not laboriously written solutions to laboriously written dilemmas but expressions of love and human friendship—as in times when the mind runs deep, on an autumn walk, in a conversation over a cup of coffee, during a time of prayer, those times in fact that he was missing most.

Many a new convert to Christ faces this in a small way in his or her family or among old friends. Their "new belief" separates them from family and friends with their "old beliefs." It is then dangerously easy to relate as a "new believer" to "unbelievers" and not as a person to people. Urged to share their faith at all costs, young Christians do so, but their motivation is often tinged with insecurity as much as it is fired by enthusiasm. As a result, they focus on the differences between believer and unbeliever rather than on the difference that belief makes. The new faith is therefore seen as a threat, and a family or a group of friends reacts by closing its ranks in a protective wall of scorn or indifference. "Silence is the worst form of persecution," wrote Pascal.[17]

Such rejection leaves the new converts downcast, with a heavy sense of having "blown it," and this may be the occasion of their first doubts. In reality, it is not their faith they are doubting, it is themselves and their ability to share their faith. Still, if they have to face much more of this, they may blame it on their faith. What is really to blame is a style of witnessing, high in emotional pressure and low in content and sensitivity, that urged them to say too much too soon and in quite the wrong manner.

All of us have our "moments," those times when our emotions are likely to run away with our trust in God—a student under the pressure of exams, a father hearing that his job is redundant, a business executive in a lonely hotel room, a mother worried about breast cancer, an author with his rejection slips, a minister struggling with jealousy over a neighbor's success, a teenager with few friends.

Seek to know yourself well enough to recognize those special times and the pressures they bring. The important thing to see in each case is that it will not be Christian truth that is under fire but your faith. When faith is in danger of being cut off by an insurgent army of emotions, it panics and loses effective contact with the faithfulness of God. This loss of contact leads to doubt.

DOWN-TO-EARTH SPIRITUALITY

What is the remedy for this variety of doubt? As with some of the other doubts, it is twofold. The immediate and short-term remedy is to give the appropriate practical solution. Beware of being side-tracked. This type of doubt is not important for what it says theologically (however wrong that may be) but for what it shows emotionally. Since the doubt is not a statement so much as a symptom, it is no use correcting what the emotions are saying. The doubter's words should be taken seriously but not literally. For what needs to be changed is what the emotions are showing, the practical root of the problem of which both the emotions and the doubt are only a result.

Interestingly, God's remedy for Elijah's depression was not a refresher course in theology but food and sleep. "An angel touched him and said, 'Rise and eat.' He looked, and there at his head was a cake baked on hot stones, and a pitcher

of water. He ate and drank and lay down again."[18] Before
God spoke to him at all, Elijah was fed twice and given a good
chance to sleep. Only then, and very gently, did God confront
him with his error.

This is always God's way. Having made us as human
beings, he respects our humanness and treats us with integrity.
That is, he treats us true to the truth of who we are. It is human
beings and not God who have made spirituality impractical.
God, the Father of Jesus Christ, numbers the hairs on our heads.
Our driving concern for food in our stomachs, for a roof over
our heads, and for love and friendship are cares to which he is no
stranger. Jesus meets us and teaches us to pray: "Give us today
our daily bread."[19] And he fleshes out his own words. He feeds
the crowds that others would dismiss, and after bringing Jairus'
daughter back from the dead, he first reminds her parents "to
give her something to eat."[20]

We, by contrast, have made spirituality impractical. The
Fall has driven a wedge between the human and the spiritual.
When we say something is "all too human," we are usually
referring to the weaker, darker side of human nature, to that
which is anything but spiritual. The spiritual has therefore
been made an escape from the real. Thus human beings who
are bound to the earth struggle to escape the animal and aspire
to become the angel. But we end by being either practical at
the expense of being spiritual or spiritual at the expense of
being practical. Paradoxically, it is God who becomes the
most down-to-earth (in the Incarnation), it is the divine that
is most truly human (in Jesus), and it is the one most truly
spiritual who is most practical.

The temptation is to keep spirituality and practicality in
conflict—or to make them mutually exclusive. Christians have
demonstrated both extremes. Some have been too "worldly"
and others too "other worldly." But the lesson of both

extremes is the same. The person who is spiritual without being practical ends in being unspiritual, and the person who is practical without being spiritual ends in being impractical. It is certainly so today. A grave weakness of current super-spirituality is its inability to be practical. In this area, for example, doubts with practical roots are often given other explanations that are sometimes simply rationalizations to cover failure to get to the practical root of the matter.

If someone is doubting because he is tired, the best remedy is not for him to pray but to sleep. If someone else is plagued with doubt because she is exhausted from overwork, what she might need is not spiritual heart-searching but a day-off in the country or three weeks in the sun. If someone is feeling "down," maybe what he or she most needs is some stiff exercise or a better diet or an evening with some friends at a hilariously funny film.

Some people are affected by weather or by a seasonal change, others by the emotional associations of a certain memory or a certain date. If there is any month in the year in which I am more "down," it is June. But this has nothing to do with horoscopes; it is simply because it is my month for hay fever. In each case, our emotions are affected by a very practical cause that needs an appropriately practical solution.

Of course, we cannot always remove the root of the problem. The anniversary date with its memories still comes round; the pollen still blows; a particular task is still daunting; but we can defuse the potential blast against faith. Obviously the discouraged Christian who is the only believer in her office cannot wave a wand and see all her colleagues converted. Nor is it usually the best answer simply to quit. But what a person can do is to recognize the emotional pressures that create the loneliness and doubt, and counterbalance this by deliberately seeking encouragement and fellowship outside work situations.

In the long run, the most practical remedy is also the most

spiritual. Whatever deals with doubt is the most helpful contribution to faith. But a solution must be appropriate as well as practical. If two people are depressed and full of doubts, perhaps only for one is the best solution a little more sleep; for the other the solution might be a little less sleep and a little more discipline in tackling the pile of letters on his desk.

In other cases still, the doubt may be compound. If so, no exclusively spiritual or practical remedy will do. Both roots must be dealt with at once. Nehemiah's reaction, facing the twin threat of an enemy attack and discouragement on his own side, illustrates this. "So we prayed to our God, and posted a guard."[21] It is not that prayer is spiritual and posting a guard is practical, though this is how we tend to talk about it. Rather, each is thoroughly practical and appropriate, and neither is sufficient without the other.

TALKING TO YOURSELF

The second part of the remedy lies in the long-term discipline of training faith so that it is not overwhelmed by moods and emotions. If we ignore this second part of the remedy and concentrate only on meeting the immediate practical need, it is easy to give the impression of pandering to indulgence. Are we to take a day off every time we feel a twinge of doubt?

The long-term remedy balances the short-term remedy and makes us less vulnerable by building up our faith where it was weak in the first place. This is the real problem. It may be comforting to think of doubt being resolved by a few nights of sleep, but it is challenging to think of faith being so weak that it could be dissolved by lack of sleep. Our faith should dictate to our emotions, not the other way around.

Oswald Chambers gives bracing counsel here:

There are certain things we must not pray about—moods for instance. Moods never go by praying, moods go by kicking. A mood nearly always has its seat in the physical condition, not in the moral. It is a continual effort not to listen to the moods which arise from a physical condition, never submit to them for a second. We have to take ourselves by the scruff of the neck and shake ourselves, and we will find that we can do what we said we could not. The curse with most of us is that we *won't*. The Christian life is one of incarnate spiritual pluck.[22]

In the same tenor, Martyn Lloyd-Jones raises a key question: "Have you realized that most of your unhappiness in life is due to the fact that you are listening to yourself instead of talking to yourself? We must talk to ourselves instead of allowing 'ourselves' to talk to us!"[23]

In listening to our emotions rather than talking to them, we fall prey to the same temptation that caught Adam and Eve off guard. The order of creation is stood on its head when the animal world (in the form of a serpent) dictates to the human world. The same thing happens when the emotions dictate to faith. The control we are called to exercise as human beings over nature is the same control we are to exercise over our own human nature. Such control comes from a disciplined faith. Pascal suggests, "We must resort to habit once the mind has seen where the truth lies, in order to steep and stain ourselves in that belief which constantly eludes us."[24]

Habits, discipline, and the formation of character—Nietzsche's "long obedience in the same direction"—are much maligned in a spontaneity-loving age like our own. But a habit need not be a rut. Habit is built-in second nature, and what is built in, whether it is a good habit or a bad habit, a dull rut or a positive strength of character, depends entirely on what we choose. Repeat an active habit and you grow strong; repeat a passive habit and you grow weak. In this case, the habit we are building is the practice of trusting God despite our feelings, so that in every situation trust becomes "second nature" to us. Faith will then be the controlling principle of our lives and not the victim of our fluctuating emotions.

The quality of our emotions depends upon the quality of our faith, just as the quality of our faith depends on the quality of our understanding. "Feeling must follow; but faith, apart from all feeling, must be there first."[25] This is Martin Luther's understanding of the relationship of faith and emotions, but he also makes clear that this is not our first nature, and it will be our second only if we carefully and patiently learn it. "The lesson of faith is a lesson that must constantly be practiced and rehearsed."[26]

Lloyd-Jones expresses this even more strongly:

> The main art in the matter of spiritual living is to know how to handle yourself. You have to take yourself in hand. You have to address yourself, preach to yourself, question yourself. The essence of this matter is to understand that this self of ours, this other man within us, has got to be handled. Do not listen to him; turn on him; speak to him; condemn him; upbraid him; exhort him; encourage him; remind him of what you know instead of placidly listening to him and allowing him to drag you down and depress you.[27]

Mastering our emotions has nothing to do with asceticism, or repression, for the purpose is not to break the emotions or deny them but to "break in" the emotions, making them teachable because they are tamed.

The Apostle Paul's example underlines again how insipid our understanding of the obedience of faith often is. Speaking of himself he writes to the Corinthians, "For my part, I run with a clear goal before me; I am like a boxer who does not beat the air; I bruise my own body and make it know its master."[28] And in case someone excuses himself or herself from submitting to Paul's rigorous standards, he adds in a letter to Thessalonica, "Each one of you must learn to gain mastery over his body."[29]

Unless we train our emotions they will lead us around by the nose, and we will be captives to every passing impulse or reaction. But once faith is trained to control the emotions and knows how to lean resolutely against weaknesses of character, another entryway of doubt is sealed shut forever.

Much of our distress as Christians comes not because of sin, but because we are ignorant of the laws of our own nature.

—Oswald Chambers

———■———

CHAPTER 9

SCARS FROM
AN OLD WOUND

Doubt from
Hidden Conflicts

Have you ever seen a small boy dreading a visit to the dentist? Or a student entering an examination insisting to everyone that he or she has no chance whatever of passing? Neither is being hopelessly pessimistic; the ploy they are using is more subtle. They are cushioning themselves against the worst that could possibly happen so that however bad it turns out to be, it will always be better than they feared.

The seventh variety of doubt is like this in having purely psychological origins. This type of doubt is so closely related to the previous one that some would make no distinction between them. But a separate look is worthwhile, for it operates at a far deeper level than emotional doubt and is inevitably more painful. Moreover, there are marked differences in the manner in which it works.

Every generation has the tendency to major in its own special insight, its own favorite discipline, its own chosen frame of reference, and to reinterpret all previous thinking in the light of this framework. For our own generation, the discipline of psychology is the leading contender for this dubious honor, and its predominance creates a situation with two equal, though opposite, dangers. Either everything is interpreted in terms of the psychological, or no interpretation in terms of the psychological is admitted. Some people, for example, see doubt as a purely psychological reality. They deny that faith has any objective basis and locate doubt in a believer's subjective ability or inability to believe. Thus they make doubt as well as belief purely a matter of psychology. On the other hand, others emphasize the element of sin, choice, and responsibility so strongly that any suggestion that psychological factors are also involved is swiftly brushed aside as an attempt to evade responsibility. The former is the psychologizing tendency and the latter the spiritualizing tendency.

A balanced understanding is more accurate and more helpful. It is as mistaken to account for objective causes of doubt by subjective explanations as to account for subjective causes by objective explanations. The doubt we are dealing with in this chapter is indeed primarily psychological, and it cannot be explained without understanding the subjective makeup of the person who is doubting.

DISBELIEVING FOR JOY

Healthy faith can be pictured as the firm, solid grip of a person who is able to reach out and grasp whatever he or she wants to hold. Imagine what it would be like, though, to grasp something firmly if you had a bad wound in the palm of your hand. The object you want to hold is still available, your muscular strength is as powerful as ever, but the pain resulting from pressure on the wound would mean that you could not comfortably exert the same strength. This is what happens in a case of this seventh type of doubt. People know they need the truth in question; they can see the difference it would make; they can even see that it is true; and they are quite able to believe it. The problem is that the very process of believing puts painful pressure on old psychological wounds that are still too sensitive to bear it or that they think are too sensitive to test. When this happens, doubt is the process and the excuse for drawing back from such a risk.

A vivid example is found in Luke's description of the evening of Resurrection Sunday. Without warning, Jesus suddenly entered the room where his disciples were assembled and confronted them with the living reality of his risen presence. Momentarily they were taken aback, caught in two minds over whether to believe, and Luke captures the curious suspension of that moment: "And while they still disbelieved for joy . . ."[1]

What a distinctive and intriguing variety of doubt this is! The average doubt is more like those mentioned earlier in the story where the disciples refused to believe that Jesus had risen when they heard the first accounts that the tomb was empty. They had no firsthand evidence, so they dismissed the initial report as an idle tale. But in doubt or not, at least they hurried to find out the truth for themselves. It was not that they believed and then doubted, but that they refused to believe without sufficient evidence. They wanted to make sure for themselves.

This later doubt, however, is different, and there was not the same excuse. More than half a day had gone by, and the evidence to confirm the first accounts had been flowing in from all sides. They heard the news reliably from the women, from the two disciples on the road to Emmaus, and from Simon Peter. Before Jesus appeared, they had already come to a conclusion: "It is true: the LORD has risen."[2] But suddenly, now that Jesus was actually right in front of them and their faith was not just a tacit agreement but a demanding reality, they disbelieved for joy. That is the uniqueness of this doubt: They disbelieved *for joy*. What they were seeing was the one thing in all the world they wanted most. That was precisely the trouble. They wanted it so much that to believe it and then discover it was false would have been profoundly disillusioning. So, instead, they preferred the safety of doubt rather than the risk of disappointment.

Can you explain this "disbelieving for joy" any other way? There was no denying that Jesus was alive. He was there as large as life, and it was quite impossible to pass it off any longer as an idle tale or an early-morning fantasy. It is not as if these men were deep-dyed skeptics or modern philosophers trained in the rigorous procedures of critical doubt. They were down-to-earth people accustomed to dealing in the hard currency of "the facts of life," people who lived naturally in a world where "seeing is believing." Yet for some reason they rejected the evidence of their own eyes and ears, and insisted on disbelieving. By doubting, they were taking out an insurance policy to cover the possible pain of any eventual disappointment.

The disciples were mature adults whose lives had been far from sheltered and reserved, yet the experience of the crucifixion had been more harrowing than any of them cared to face again. Any hopes they might have tried to salvage from the wreckage of those fateful days must have looked forlorn. All around them lay the debris of shattered dreams. Hour after hour, over and over again, they must have rerun the events in their minds. But at the end of every possible train of thought was the stark finality of a bloody cross and a sealed tomb. And then, at last, the gaping wound that was their memory must have slowly begun to heal; their thoughts must have started to turn naturally toward resuming their lives.

That was the moment when Jesus appeared, and he caught them on the raw before the sedative of passing time had dulled the pain. He stood before them, the sum of all they wanted. But for the sheer joy of what it would mean if true, they refused to believe in case it might not be. What they were saying in their doubt is that it was too good to be true, and this way they adroitly protected the wound and refused to risk reopening it. The one fact that they wanted became the one fact too much, so they disbelieved for joy.

This doubt comes from the fear of being hurt where we have the scars from an old psychological wound. It is one to which many of us are prone. Are not most of us wounded at some point? Don't we all have deep conflicts that are unresolved, perhaps unacknowledged? It is not necessarily that we have con-flicts and scars that stand out publicly, livid and unhealed, but that even if our wounds are invisible, we know they are there, and we instinctively know the pain that pressure on them brings.

Sometimes even the memory of previous pain at a particu-lar point is enough to summon up the pain again. This means that though we have come to believe in Christ and have grown into a deep conviction of faith, there is still one place sealed off, one place where healing is not allowed, one place where we shy away from complete openness. So if to trust involves opening up, if to believe means laying ourselves open, if to love is to make ourselves vulnerable, then rather than taking the risk of faith, we choose to doubt.

POLITE BUT SELF-DEFEATING

There are two features of this type of doubt. The first is its style of argument and tone of voice. Here, there is no discontented grumbling or sharp intellectual criticism, such as is common in the other doubts that also are rationalizations. Initially, in fact, this doubt can look so appealing and sound so polite that it is hardly recognizable as doubt. The heart of its case is the claim that God's word is too good to be true. Indeed the New English Bible translates the verse as, "They were still unconvinced, still wondering, for it seemed too good to be true." But this is put forward with such unassuming deference that it sounds more like a compliment, and it seems churlish to consider it even a veiled criticism.

The suggestion of doubt can be expressed in a gloomy, unbudging melancholy or in an excited, trembling joy, as if the person was longing to reach out his hand and take for himself or herself yet does not dare do so. But the effect is the same. While such doubters rarely hesitate to see that someone else might benefit, they say in effect, "It is too good to be true for me." The doubters sound humble when they suggest they are unworthy of such a wonderful truth, but this humility is only a smoke screen to conceal the deeper problem: They are not so much unworthy as unwilling.

In almost every instance, the person is challenged to believe at the very point where he or she most needs and most wants to believe. This is not a coincidence. The psychological hurt of the doubt comes from the clash between the desire to believe and the fear to believe as they meet head-on right over the old wound. The doubter claims that the trouble with God's truth is that it is more desirable than credible. But neither the desirability nor the credibility of the matter are the problem. What matters to the doubter is that the wound remains covered and protected. So what would otherwise be eminently desirable and entirely credible must be dismissed. It is done with a show of reluctance, but the dismissal is no less decisive.

A second feature of this doubt is that it is self-defeating. Here lies its special sadness; no one is hurt more than the doubter. Afraid to believe what they want to believe, they fail to believe what they need to believe, and they alone are the losers. With some doubts, the issue rises at points that are not central to faith. They are taken seriously at once only because it is the style and integrity of faith-with-understanding to do so. But this doubt is different. The issue raised does not lie on the circumference of life but at its very center. Whether it is solved is not a matter of indifference to faith but a matter of life and death.

Most other rationalizing doubts are self-serving. The issues they raise are viewed as welcome excuses. If doubt is pressed, faith can be thrown over for what looks like freedom. But if this type of doubt is a rationalization, it is not a glib one, and its outcome is not more freedom but more frustration. The doubters are doubtful where they would most like to be certain. They hang back at the one moment they would most like to step forward. They shrug their shoulders when they long to embrace. They reject what they are dying to accept.

DO I HAVE A PROBLEM OR
DOES A PROBLEM HAVE ME?

What has happened to create this doubt is that a problem (such as a deep conflict or a bad experience) has been allowed to usurp God's place and become the controlling principle of life. Instead of viewing the problem from the vantage point of faith, the doubter views faith from the vantage point of the problem. Instead of faith *sizing up* the problem, the situation ends with the problem *scaling down* faith. The world of faith is upside down, and in the topsy-turvy reality of doubt, a problem has *become god* and God has *become a problem.*

This is exactly why the doubt is self-defeating, for whatever takes God's place (whatever becomes an ultimately decisive influence) must be taken with ultimate seriousness. And if we think about it, we see that the only problem that can be taken with ultimate seriousness is an *unanswerable problem,* an enduring problem to which no answer has ever—or perhaps, must ever—be found. Only the unanswerable problem is big enough to *play god* for us psychologically. As soon as a problem is answered, it is reduced to size and can no longer be taken with ultimate seriousness.

This is why people who are apt to define themselves in terms of their problems will do so only in terms of large problems (or small problems that have assumed large proportions). If a problem is small, then psychologically speaking I can say, "I have a problem." But the greater the problem becomes, the more it is likely to reach the point where psychologically speaking I should say, "The problem has me."

"I am the LORD your God. . . . You shall have no other gods to set against me"[3] is not only a principle of correct theology but of sound psychology. Whatever assumes in our lives a practical importance that is greater than God will *become god* to us. And since we become what we worship, to let an unanswerable problem *become god* to us is the surest way to guarantee that life will be characterized at its heart by defeat. When we listen to this doubt we are wheeling a Trojan horse into our camp. Doubt claims to offer the best protection against pain, but, in fact, it becomes the sole bar to healing. It introduces itself as the best insurance agent to cover the risk of faith, but it protects faith at the cost of smothering it. As Shakespeare put it in *Measure for Measure:*

> *Our doubts are traitors*
> *And make us lose the good we oft might win*
> *By fearing to attempt.*[4]

At worst such doubts do more. Not only is it in their power to fear, but in their insistence on their supremacy they create the facts they fear. This particular doubt works out this way because experience has been made into an absolute—and bad—experience at that. So the decisive influence in life is not God but a bad experience that colors the rest of life. "It is often the case," writes Augustine, "that a man who had had experience of a bad doctor is afraid to trust himself even to a good one."[5] After an experience with a bad doctor, it would be reasonable to check the credentials of every subsequent doctor but ridiculous to reject all doctors completely. Cheated once with a counterfeit bank note, it is only sensible to keep an eye open for future fraud, but to refuse to use any money at all would be silly. Yet this, in effect, is the self-defeating logic of this doubt.

PUDDLEGLUM AND HIS PAST

With some people, such doubt is almost a matter of temperament, whether this is a result of heredity or environment or the outcome of their own brooding reflections. With others, it is a characteristic that appears from time to time. Like A. A. Milne's "Eeyore" or C. S. Lewis's incomparably gloomy but loyal "Puddleglum," such people can always be relied on to see the dark side of everything. After a week with six days of sunshine, they will remember the one day of rain. Life has its pleasures, its joys, and its success, but somehow the good things seem to happen to everyone but them.

It is not that people like this are killjoys, unhappy because others are happy, for they are genuinely happy for others. But they seem to be happy for others mainly because it proves that things like that don't happen to them. The happiness of their unhappiness is its reliability. The unhappiness of happiness is its risk. If they are ever offered what they want, the strength of their desire can be gauged by the speed in which they spot the snag. If this person says that something is too good to be true, you can take it that they see it as both good and true but, for some hidden reason, not allowed to be so for them.

What would you think of someone who won the lottery after a lifetime of trying but who took the ticket to his next-door neighbor saying he is sure he must have heard the number wrongly? It is exactly what he wants. After all, he has been attempting to win it for years, but when it finally happens it's too good to be true. "Better not get too excited. Better not dwell on it. There's always the pleasure of trying again." Finally he settles for the fun of hoping to win rather than the fun of winning. We would shake our heads in amazement if we knew someone who acted like this. But the logic of the doubt we are discussing is no less silly, though far more understandable.

With other people this doubt is not a question of temperament but the result of a particular experience or a deep, perhaps unacknowledged conflict in their lives. Ours is a violent generation—wounded and wounding—and there are few people whom life has given no injury capable of producing such a doubt. I have a friend whose whole life cries out for God's love as father but whose desire for God's love as father is checkmated by an overriding fear of God's love. And the root of this lies not only in his experience of the cruelly twisted relationship that was his father's "love" but in his adamant refusal to consider forgiving his father. So God's love continues to be "too good to be true" for him. But what was once a winsome, entirely understandable doubt has degenerated into a self-pitying rationalization, a poorly constructed facade to cover a festering wound. The trouble is not that God's trustworthiness is the least bit undesirable or incredible but that to trust God is to risk an openness that would pry loose his right to his grievance and so remove his right to self-pity.

Sometimes this sort of doubt requires a skilled counselor or professional psychiatrist to open up and resolve the conflict at its base. But such doubt is even more common at less serious levels. Many examples spring to mind. A philosophically minded woman, for example, trembles on the verge of faith, keenly desiring to believe God's truth that is the goal of her life's search but considers it too good to be true. She does not doubt because it is any less good or true than she might wish but because her experience of Christians to this point has shown a "leap of faith" so suicidal to her mind that her integrity shudders at the thought. There is no doubt which of the two she wants, and the point is not really which of the two is true. She disbelieves for joy because she is afraid to run the risk.

Most of us know something of this in ourselves. With some of us, the wound is a childhood experience. With others, the memory of a previous marriage. With yet others, the result of an experience of particular shame or fear or hurt. All of us have our painful memories, and it is when the call to faith puts pressure on an unacknowledged conflict or unhealed memory that we balk, preferring the comfort of doubt to the risky business of trusting.

Some people, for example, have a deep anxiety about God as they do about all of life; going back to an experience of being abandoned or abused in their past. Others suffer from fearfulness and an inability to hand control to God, rooted in a weak sense of self. Still others close themselves off from their feelings by developing an aggressively activist or intellectualist faith—and then find they are vulnerable to doubt when their busyness is halted in its tracks or their rational proofs for God are trumped by objections their reason cannot answer. Others again are perfectionists who cannot feel God's love unless they feel they have *done* something to win it; unconditional love of any sort is beyond their understanding.

In each case, past history has become decisive in the way people believe. Their doubt is not because of philosophical questions but psychological experiences. I'm not saying that people like this are gloomy, as if the whole of their lives were overcast like a leaden sky. Far from it. Quite often they are not the slightest bit gloomy or hesitant about anything— except at the particular point where the old wound still festers or the scar is still tender. In all other points, they are only too glad to respond readily in faith to any challenge or promise which God gives.

This is perhaps why it is often such a surprise to stumble on "the one point." It is so different from what we imagine, so against the grain of what we were led to expect. Why is it that an apparently placid searcher passes through a place of violent cynicism and hostility just before he believes? Why is it that a girl who obviously wants to get married becomes most negative just after a proposal? The reason is that each is struggling intensely as the desire to believe and the fear to believe clash like a psychological implosion right over an old wound. What each is doing in that moment is "disbelieving for joy."

LONG-TERM AND SHORT-TERM REMEDIES

Is there a remedy for this subtle form of doubt? At first we might wonder, for any obvious solution is circular and therefore as self-defeating as the doubt itself. To be told to "believe" when we doubt is as unhelpful as being told to "cheer up" when we are depressed or to "join in" when we are feeling alienated from everyone around us. The doubt may look ridiculous to faith, since from faith's point of view doubt is refusing what faith most wants to believe. But the straightforward solution looks equally ridiculous to doubt, for from doubt's point of view it is having to believe what it least wants to believe. So another way must be found, a way that bypasses the essential circularity of this type of doubt.

This doubt, like others, must be solved on its own terms. If someone is doubting because he is no longer thankful to God and has quite ignored the "once and might have been" (as we saw in Chapter 3), then no amount of intellectual discussion will touch his problem. Equally, if someone is doubting because she has no basis for faith, then no amount of stirring reminders or encouragements will be a substitute for the necessary intellectual understanding. Basically, though, psychologically-rooted doubts can be resolved in a similar way to the emotionally-rooted doubts, for their cause too is subjective. The initial wound was objective and real, of course, yet the doubt is caused, not by the wound itself but by the way it was regarded and the place it was given. These are a matter of subjective choice, so the remedy must be directed accordingly. Moreover, both types of doubt can be best helped with long-term and short-term remedies.

The long-term problem is unhealed conflicts and wounds, and these need healing so that faith is able to come into its own. The best long-term remedy lies in remembering that God is light and that we are called to "walk in the light as he himself is in the light."[6] We should practice a style of openness in our relationships to God and those closest to us. This openness will not only mean constant forgiveness for our sins, but openness and honesty (and therefore healing) about our conflicts and our wounds. If this is our practice, we will be letting God be God over our conflicts, wounds, and sorrows as well as our sins—in short, over all our problems.

What is promised in the cross is not some "cheap miracle" or "instant cure." To speak of healing is to speak of a deep and radical surgery in the human heart. With some people the healing is almost complete; with others the improvement is substantial. But whatever the case, the essential point is satisfied. What leads to doubt is not so much the pain of a wound in itself, as the memory of a wound that is clung to. It is not the unhealed wound but the wound that is never allowed to heal, the conflict that is not acknowledged. The wound that is completely healed no longer provides a potential opening for doubt, and the wound that is substantially healed need not if the strength gained from healing is coupled with a realistic understanding of how, when, and where the doubt may strike again.

The solution is not easy on the short-term level either, but two things are useful to remember when helping anyone who is experiencing this doubt. The first, as always, is the importance of identifying the doubt. It is the nameless doubt that is most damaging to the mind. Unidentified, perhaps unidentifiable, it lurks below the conscious mind like a waiting shark, and there is no limit to its shadowy potential for destruction. As the Chinese proverb runs, "The doubting mind sees many ghosts." So be sure to identify the doubt, name it, bring it sharply into focus, and exorcise its ghosts. Be specific about what it is and about what it isn't. This in itself does not deal with the doubt, but it helps the doubter to see it for what it is and prevents it from being more damaging than it need be.

Being specific is especially important for this type of doubt because it has no objective cause. It poses no final objection to faith, only an immediate objection to believing. Once the doubter understands this, the whole complexion of the problem is altered. The problem does not lie in what they believe, or even in how they believe, but in who they are as believers. It is one thing for someone to see that a problem is "entirely his own," for a person can well see this, shrug his shoulders, and walk away from it. But it is quite another to realize that it is in his own highest interests to solve it as quickly as possible. The danger is not that the person doubts that there is any truth but that he should persuade himself that he doesn't need it. To identify this doubt, therefore, puts the responsibility squarely on the doubter.

GHOSTS DON'T EAT BREAKFAST

Second, it is helpful to remember that the circularity of the doubt is best met by short-circuiting it. The doubt is entirely logical, but the circle of its logic rests on premises that are too restricted. Since a conflict or a wound and not words are at the heart of the problem, what is needed is not fresh arguments so much as fresh air. The doubter's facts are not complete, and he or she has not examined them for a long time. What he or she needs is a fresh context that makes all believing entirely natural, sheds light on the wider situation, and throws the known facts into a different perspective.

The answer to bad humor is not to say "cheer up" but to tell a good joke. We can be so depressed that the set of our minds and hearts is against laughing and false humor only entices a grimace. But given the right joke, the creative power of humor is such that the lightning speed of involuntary laughter will escape the most determined heart and mind, and people laugh before they think of it. It is the same with this doubt. The answer it needs is to be shown something that it is utterly natural to believe.

Jesus did this with the disciples. They refused to believe the evidence of their own eyes, but he didn't rebuke them or dazzle them with supernatural signs. He simply took some fish and ate it in front of them. They were surprised into belief, coaxed back gently, rebuked by the utterly natural and simple. After all, this was what they had seen him do a thousand times. "Ghosts don't eat breakfast!" was what convinced them Jesus was alive.

Meet doubt head-on with a solution in the order of "Believe, don't doubt" and all you do is face one simplistic, short-sighted argument with another, and one that is cold and comfortless at that. Instead, point out gently what doubters are doing when they doubt and introduce them to the infinite sufficiency of God who is himself the answer. Put your answer in words and "give it flesh" in terms of compassion and patience. Then you will find that the understanding of God's truth will bring its own creative self-realization, a flooding awareness that releases repentance and faith and short circuits the small-mindedness of doubt.

Like a theater audience suddenly aware that it is being watched by another audience, everything suddenly changes for the person who doubts. Moments earlier the doubter was king in the tiny realm of the problem, asking only whether he or she could believe in God. Suddenly the question is wider, and doubters find themselves on their knees being asked whether God can believe in them. As God is seen for who he is, the terms of the problem change and the sources of the problem dissolve. The mysterious change of heart and mind is the Holy Spirit's gift of repentance and faith.

When this doubt goes and faith comes back into its own, the wonder that faith then knows is in direct proportion to the absurdity of the doubt beforehand. Far from being too good to be true, there is nothing so good and nothing else so true. God proves not only better to us than our worst fears but better to us than our wildest dreams. "Disbelieving for joy" is quickly followed by being "surprised by joy."

PART THREE

■|

TWO TORTURING
QUESTIONS

CHAPTER 10

WHY, O LORD?

Doubt from Inquisitiveness

So far we have looked at the character of doubt (Part One) and we have looked at seven of the basic categories of doubt (Part Two). But perhaps to some people's surprise and disappointment, we have not looked at any specific doubts. In particular, we have not looked at two doubts that are so common and so profound that no discussion of doubt is complete without them. These two doubts grow out of two little questions that have proved torturous to faith: "Why, O Lord?" and "How long, O Lord?"

The first of the doubts is the doubt of impatient inquisitiveness—or as it might be called, "keyhole theology." Think of detective stories and the importance of keyholes in the days before electronic eavesdropping. Far more than a mere security device, a keyhole was a unique source of information. Without it, what lay behind the heavy door was a mystery. With it, a glimpse into the room was possible and so was a chance to hear the conversation inside. Many a criminal trial, at least in novels, turned upon the evidence of a keyhole.

But keyholes can be as misleading as they are useful. The few words overheard may be vital, but what if you don't know the context that explained them? What if there is a mysterious other person in the conversation, sitting just out of sight? Who is he? What is he saying? Use the very incomplete evidence of the keyhole to jump to a wrong conclusion and you may be further off track than if there is no keyhole at all.

Franz Kafka captures this uncertainty in *The Castle*. Minor servants were growing desperate after forlorn, lifelong attempts to get beyond the impersonal outer circle of castle bureaucracy. To compensate for their loss of dignity and hope, they fell back on a fantasy world of absurdly involved and pathetic explanations, a world where guesswork stood in for knowledge, where elaborate arguments were built on silences and firm conclusions were drawn from a glance or a raised eyebrow.

As the hero K says to Pepi, "You chambermaids are used to spying through keyholes and from that you get this way of thinking, of drawing conclusions, as grand as they are false about the whole situation from some little thing you really see."[1]

That is the trouble with keyholes. You don't always see enough to come to a conclusion, but once you've seen a little it's difficult to resist trying. This mistake is the essence of the doubt of keyhole theology. There are times when we see glimpses of God's ways but not enough to allow us to make true conclusions about what he is doing and why. But we cannot resist jumping to conclusions anyway.

Then, being insistent as well as inquisitive, we refuse to suspend judgment, and our wrong conclusions so misrepresent God that we end by doubting him.

SUSPEND JUDGMENT, NOT THINKING

What does it mean for faith to suspend judgment? Could this be a disguised form of irrationality smuggled in at a late hour? Perhaps doubt is a problem of too much thinking after all? Emphatically not. We have surely laid to rest the hoary rumor that doubt is a problem of too much thinking. Most doubts, as we have seen, have far more to do with wrong thinking or no thinking at all than with too much thinking. In each case a genuinely critical, mature way of thinking has an essential role to play in moving toward the remedy. To think and not understand is one problem; not to think and have no chance of understanding is a greater one. A keen mind will rarely remain idle and satisfied. If the faith by which it lives does not allow it room to move, the mind is apt to exact its own revenge. A good mind denied by bad faith will self-destruct with insecurity, guilt, fanaticism, or doubt.

The Christian wholeheartedly supports genuine rationality. But we must add a qualification to give this balance. The Christian faith is second to none in the place it gives to reason, but it is also second to none in keeping reason in its place. We never know the value of a thing until we know its limits. Put unlimited value on something and in the end you will exhaust it of all value. This is as true of reason as it is of natural resources such as oil.

This is why the Christian faith is thoroughly rational but not the least bit rationalistic. It is also why rationalism—and not Christian faith—leads to irrationality. If we forget the limits of a thing, we fly in the face of reality and condemn ourselves to learn the simple ironic lesson: More without limits is less; less with limits is more.

We have emphasized all along that the Christian faith is a warranted belief and therefore profoundly rational. This means that we have sure and sufficient reasons at the point of coming to know God (the point of original assent), but this is not the case for every subsequent question in life. Human beings are finite and the world is now fallen, so life will contain many mysteries that are opaque to a searcher, however curious or persistent he or she is. At such times we see through a glass darkly or, as it were, through a keyhole partially. It is not that it is rational to come to believe and irrational to continue to believe, as if the break between rationality and irrationality were a matter of time and stages. Rather the truth is this: We always have sure and sufficient reasons for knowing why we can trust God, but do not always know what God is doing and why.

Put differently, the rationality of faith is implacably opposed to absurdity. But it has no quarrel with mystery; it can tell the difference between the two. The Christian faith's contention with rationalism is not that it has too much reason in it, but that it has very little else. When Christian believers come to faith their understanding and their trust go hand in hand, but as they continue in faith their trust may sometimes be called to go on by itself without their understanding.

That is where the principle of suspended judgment applies. If the Christian's faith is to be itself and let God be God at such times, it must suspend judgment and say, "Father, I do not understand you, but I trust you."

Notice what this means. Christians do not say, "I do not understand you at all, but I trust you anyway." Rather we say, "I do not understand you *in this situation*, but I *understand why I trust you anyway*. Therefore I can trust that you understand even though I don't." The former is a mystery unrelieved by rationality and indistinguishable from absurdity; the latter is a statement of the rationality of faith walking hand in hand with the mystery of faith.

Suspending judgment is not unique to Christians. There

is a Jewish story of the prophet Elijah on a journey with the Rabbi Jachanan.

They walked all day, and at nightfall they came to the humble cottage of a poor man, whose only treasure was a cow. The poor man ran out of his cottage, and his wife ran too, to welcome the strangers for the night and to offer them all of the simple hospitality that they were able to give in straitened circumstances. Elijah and the Rabbi were entertained with plenty of the cow's milk, sustained by home-made bread and butter, and they were put to sleep in the best bed while their kindly hosts lay down before the kitchen fire. But in the morning the poor man's cow was dead. . . .

They walked all the next day, and came that evening to the house of a very wealthy merchant, whose hospitality they craved. The merchant was cold and proud and rich, and all that he would do for the prophet and his companion was to lodge them in a cowshed and feed them on bread and water. In the morning, however, Elijah thanked him very much for what he had done, and sent for a mason to repair one of his walls, which happened to be falling down, as a return for his kindness.

The Rabbi Jachanan, unable to keep silence any longer, begged the holy man to explain the meaning of his dealings with human beings.

"In regard to the poor man who received us so hospitably," replied the prophet, "it was decreed that his wife was to die that night, but in reward for his goodness, God took the cow instead of the wife. I repaired the wall of the rich miser because a chest of gold was concealed near the place, and if the miser had repaired the wall himself, he would have discovered the treasure.

"Say not therefore to the Lord: What doest thou? But say in thy heart: Must not the Lord of all the earth do right?"

Indeed, we should all say that in our hearts. So the principle of suspended judgment is not irrational. It is not a leap of faith but a walk of faith. As believers we cannot always know why, but *we can always know why we trust God who knows why*, and that makes all the difference.

HE WHO KNOWS WHY CAN BEAR ANY HOW

The snag with the principle of suspended judgment is obvious: What is eminently reasonable in theory is rather more difficult in practice. In practice, the pressure of mystery acts on faith like sandpaper on a wound. It isn't just that we would like to know what we do not know but that we feel we must know what we cannot know. The one produces frustration because curiosity is denied; the other leads to anguish. More specifically, the poorer our understanding is in coming to faith the more we need to understand everything after coming to faith. If we do not know why we trust God in the beginning, then we will always need to know exactly what God is doing in order to trust him. Failing to grasp that, we may not be able to continue trusting him, for anything we do not understand may count decisively against what we are able to trust.

If, on the other hand, we do know why we trust God, we will be able to trust him in situations where we do not understand what he is doing. For what God is doing may be ambiguous, but it will not be inherently contradictory. It may be mystery to us, but mystery is only inscrutable; what would be insufferable is absurdity.

Let's change the picture from a detective story to a wartime situation. In a fallen world, Christians are in the same position as patriots in a country occupied by a foreign power; in "enemy territory," as C. S. Lewis described it. If they resist, they face not only the enemy but the torturing questions raised by the moral ambiguities in the only style of opposition open to them.

The anomalies and dilemmas of this are captured in the philosopher Basil Mitchell's celebrated parable of the resistance fighter:

> In time of war in an occupied country, a member of the resistance meets one night a Stranger who deeply impresses him. They spend that night together in conversation. The Stranger tells the partisan that he himself is on the side of the resistance—indeed that he is in command of it, and urges the partisan to have faith in him no matter what happens. The partisan is utterly convinced at that meeting of the Stranger's sincerity and constancy and undertakes to trust him.
>
> They never meet in conditions of intimacy again. But sometimes the Stranger is seen helping members of the resistance, and the partisan is grateful and says to his friends "He is on our side." Sometimes he is seen in the uniform of the police handing over patriots to the occupying power. On these occasions his friends murmur against him: but the partisan still says, "He is on our side." He still believes that, in spite of appearances, the Stranger did not deceive him. Sometimes he asks the Stranger for help and receives it. He is then thankful. Sometimes he asks and does not receive it. Then he says, "The Stranger knows best."[2]

A situation like this is not easy for wartime faith, and talk of the difference between ambiguity and contradiction is apt to sound academic and comfortless. Other questions matter much more. Is God really on our side? How can we tell when he is in disguise? Isn't it dangerously confusing if he seems to dress up as the enemy? Why does he sometimes appear to be flying the wrong flag? Surely we cannot *only* trust? Don't we also need to know? What if we have been duped, deceived, led into a trap, betrayed? Can we trust a God who seems to behave like a divine Pimpernel, popping up in the strangest of disguises, using the most paradoxical of means? Unless he shows some stability or continuity that we can see, how can we rely on him, how can he be counted on? How can we know he is different from the Eastern notion of god that turns life's reality into a fancy dress ball and human personalities into multi-million disguises and fantasies of the divine? In short, how do we know God can be trusted?

THE RESISTANCE LEADER KNOWS BEST

At the root there are only two basic problems for faith—the existence of God and the character of God. Is God there? Is God good? But it is precisely the answers to these questions that the mystery of evil mauls most savagely. If faith is not strong enough to suspend judgment, it will have to press reason and logic too far and create such a distortion of God in its own mind that either this god would be the devil (Charles Baudelaire's charge) or else the only excuse for such a god would be that he doesn't exist (Stendahl's charge).

In its strongest form, many atheists use the alleged contradictions of God's justice in an evil world to justify their atheism. "The idea of God is the sole wrong for which I cannot forgive mankind," wrote the Marquis de Sade.[3] But this is also the dilemma of the believer in the abnormal situation of the fallen world. Expressing the crisis of meaning that exile in Babylon meant for the faithful Jews, Jeremiah used this very picture: "The LORD played an enemy's part and overwhelmed Israel."[4]

What is the difference between God disguising himself and deceiving us? That is where the principle of suspended judgment operates. Face to face with mystery, and especially the mystery of evil, the faith that understands why it has come to trust must trust where it has not come to understand. Faith does not know why in terms of the *immediate*, but it knows why it trusts God who knows why in terms of the *ultimate*.

In other words, the Lord of all the earth does right. The resistance leader knows best. He may look like an unkind friend, an unjust judge, and an uncaring father—as Jesus suggested. But he is not. He can be trusted through thick and thin because he is not a stranger but a friend. Jesus said to his disciples before his crucifixion, "You do not understand now what I am doing, but one day you will."[5]

So it is not irrational for us to suspend judgment in these situations. Doing so stems from sufficient understanding, and it will result in complete understanding. For the moment we need not insist. We can trust. At such times everything around us will pressure us or call on us to make judgments. The situation we face may be riddled with apparent contradictions, but since we know that not all the facts are available, we are not only wrong but foolish to make judgments and press reason too far. As Martin Luther advised, in such situations, "Faith should close its eyes and should not judge or decide according to what it feels or sees."[6]

Two aspects of suspending judgment must be emphasized. First, we must never confuse it with an embargo on asking questions. There is nothing wrong with raising questions, pursuing possible answers, and searching for evidence. All these are processes of thought that stop short of making judgments. The problem is not that the judgments of faith are themselves improper, let alone blasphemous, for judgments are part and parcel of the thinking process that God has given us. The problem in this situation is not that we make judgments on God but that we make judgments at all when we have insufficient grounds on which to do so. Once again it is not the result of too much thinking but of the wrong sort of thinking.

Notice also how the fallacy of making an unfounded judgment grows into the blasphemy of making a judgment on God. The temptation to doubt does not come in *not believ-*

ing God but in believing what is *not* God. The danger is that we press judgment too far and our speculation creates such a distorted picture of God that we cannot continue to believe in good faith. Believing the wrong thing is always halfway to believing nothing. Our misrepresentations of God are so pathetically inadequate or monstrously hideous that to believe in him any longer is unnecessary or repugnant. C. S. Lewis was able to recognize this even in the middle of his grief.

> Not that I am (I think) in much danger of ceasing to believe in God. The real danger is in coming to believe such dreadful things about Him. The conclusion I dread is not "so there is no God after all" but "so this is what God is really like. Deceive yourself no longer."[7]

IN THE ABSENCE OF GUIDANCE

There are two situations that make it especially difficult to suspend judgment. The first is when it seems that God is not guiding us, or we cannot make out what God is doing. If we are honest, we all know times when God seems unpredictable. In one situation, someone disobeys God and the whole human race suffers; in another, someone disobeys God and all is forgiven. Or two people fall ill and one dies but the other recovers. Or again sometimes we feel God's closeness, and sometimes we feel left on our own.

Of course, if we were able to be more logical under pressure, the question would not be "Can God guide me?" or "Has God guided me?" but "Is God guiding me *now*?" However, the thrust of the predicament is so immediate and so insistent that the logical distinction is blurred. If it seems that God is not guiding me now and if this is sufficiently painful, it is easy to forget that he has guided before and not to wonder if he is able to guide at all.

The pressure is painful because of the feeling that God is not guiding us at the very moment when so much is at stake. If his honor is not in question, than at least our lives and reputations are. Everything in us becomes very emphatic. We need to know in order to decide We cannot juggle factors indefinitely or delay a decision forever. It's embarrassing to be unable to answer the inquiries of our friends. It's demoralizing to lose a sense of direction and feel we are drifting. Have we missed the way by mistake? Have we done something wrong?

There is no end to such haunting questions, and the longer they are unanswered, the louder they mock. Faith tosses and turns like someone delirious in a fever. Everything has become unreal, nothing is impossible. Doesn't God care? Is God there after all or have we been mistaken all along? Everything screams at us to choose, to decide, to act, just to do something. If only there were a word, a sign, a token, anything at all from God to help. But there is only silence and impenetrable darkness.

Bunyan's Pilgrim experienced the same temptation when Atheist mocked him about his journey to the Celestial City. Hearing that he was heading for Mt. Zion, Atheist roared with laughter and Christian was shaken by his explanation:

CHRISTIAN: "What is the meaning of your laughter?"
ATHEIST: "I laugh to see what ignorant persons you are, to take upon you so tedious a journey and yet are like to have nothing but travel for your pains."
CHRISTIAN: "Why man? Do you think we shall not be received?"
ATHEIST: "Received! There is no such place as you dream of in all the world."[8]

Scorn is a deadly argument and Atheist's taunt makes Christian wonder. But Bunyan's point is not only that skepticism can stir doubts in a believer but that every believer has his own private skeptic sitting in on the inner counsels of his heart. For long periods the skeptic-in-us may be silent, voted down in argument or quieted by reason, but give him just a few moments of uncertainty over guidance and he will be up on his feet again, questioning vociferously. Are we really being guided as we thought? How do we know we're on the right track? Is there any such destination as the place we think we're going to?

Here faith simply has to suspend judgment on what God is doing. Faith does not know why, but it knows why it trusts God who knows why. We do not trust God because he guides us; we trust God and then are guided, which means that we can trust God even when we do not seem to be guided. Faith may be in the dark about guidance, but it is never in the dark about God. What God is doing may be mystery, but who God is is not. So faith can remain itself and retain its integrity by suspending judgment.

Jesus underwrites such faith when he promises, "I am the light of the world. No follower of mine shall wander in the dark."[9] He does not say we will never *walk* in the dark, but that we do not *wander* in the dark or have a way of life at home in darkness. To anyone not knowing the anguish of such a situation, the distinction may sound trivial—the darkness appears as dark and the dilemma as agonizing. But neither is ultimate, for the outcome lies with God. Oswald Chambers explains: "When I am going on with God in His path, I do not understand, but God does; therefore I understand God, not His path."[10]

This tough trust has been the experience of countless believers who have suspended judgment although they did not know the whys and wherefores of God's guidance. Part of Job's dilemma was at this point:

If I go forward, he is not there;
   if backward, I cannot find him;
when I turn left I do not descry him;
   I face right, but I see him not.
But he knows me in action or at rest;
   When he tests me, I prove to be gold.
My feet have kept to the path he has set me.[11]

David writes, "Even though I walk through a valley dark as death I fear no evil, for thou art with me."[12] But perhaps the most illuminating biblical example is Isaiah's challenge:

Which of you fears the Lord and obeys
   his servant's commands?
The man who walks in dark places with no light,
   yet trusts in the name of the Lord and leans on his God.
But you who kindle a fire and set fire-brands alight,
   go, walk into your own fire.[13]

The believer who trusts God and suspends judgment is contrasted with the person who cannot trust God and therefore must create his or her own light with self-made sparks rather than trust God and wait in the dark. Jeremiah speaks of the same predicament: "It was I whom he [God] led away and left to walk in darkness, where no light is."[14] As Oswald Chambers says, "Are you in the dark just now in your circumstances, or in your life with God? Then remain quiet. If you open your mouth in the dark, you will talk in the wrong mood: darkness is the time to listen."[15]

A situation like this is easy from every perspective except the inside—and that, unfortunately, is the one that counts. The menace is negligible when anticipated in theory or remembered in the past—no worse than a fog rolling back in the sun or a nightmare that recedes when we wake. Everything is so obvious afterward. God's ways are not our ways. God's thoughts really are higher than our thoughts. That is when we can say with Augustine, "You were guiding me as a helmsman steers a ship, but the course you steered was beyond my understanding."[16] But the hard question is whether we can say, "Father, I do not understand you, but I trust you" while we are *still in the darkness*. That is the challenge faith faces in suspending judgment and that is the time doubt raises its voice.

IN TIMES OF SUFFERING

The second situation is even more devastating—the experience of suffering. Pain and suffering, whether physical or mental, can be considered from many angles, all of which should be adequately explained to give a comprehensive answer to the questions they raise. But our interest here is not with ultimate metaphysical questions nor with wider practical approaches in facing suffering but with the narrower question of the doubt that we experience when we trust God and suspend judgment.

Suffering is the most acute trial that faith can face, and the questions it raises are the sharpest, the most insistent, and the most damaging that faith will meet. Here as nowhere else is the supreme challenge to suspend judgment. The basic principle is the same (we do not know why, but we know why we trust God who knows why), and our basic prayer is the same ("Father, I do not understand you, but I trust you"), but the price we are asked to pay here is unique. Imagine all that lies behind these words of a Jewish prisoner in the Second World War.

> *I believe in the sun even when it is not shining.*
> *I believe in love even when I cannot feel it.*
> *I believe in God, even when he is silent.*[17]

Can faith bear the pain and still trust God, suspending judgment and resting in the knowledge that God is there, God is good, and God knows best? Or will the pain be so great that only meaning will make it endurable so that reason must be pressed further and further and judgments must be made? To suspend judgment not only seems hard but ridiculous. At first it makes the problem worse. To suffer is one thing, to suffer without meaning is another, but to suffer and choose not to press for any meaning is worst of all. Yet that is the suicidal submission that faith's suspension of judgment seems to involve.

As suffering continues, the fire heats, the temperature mounts, the pressure increases, and the unbearable anguish threatens to choke faith and turn its cry into a scream of doubt. To suspend judgment and to simply trust is the hardest thing. Faith must reach deep into its reserves of courage and endurance if the rising panic of incomprehensible pain is not to be overwhelming.

In Job we have the world's classic sufferer, the one in whom every sufferer knows he or she has at least one brother. But much of Job's agony was that he was racked by this very dilemma. Was he to trust God and suspend judgment, or was he to doubt in pressing for an explanation? At first he passed the test with honors. Disaster hit him, his children were killed and his fortunes ruined, but his faith in God remained underterred. "Throughout all this Job did not sin; he did not charge God with unreason."[18] Job did not know why, but he knew why he trusted God who knew why—and in suspending judgment, he trusted. The resistance leader knew what he was doing.

But this, of course, was only the first round of the testing and, as events unfolded, agony was piled on agony and there was no relief. Job's wife urged him to curse God and die, his friends slandered him falsely and heartlessly, his brothers held aloof, his relatives faded away, his servants forgot him, his slaves refused to answer him, children despised him, and he came to stink in the nostrils of his own family.[19] Above all, he felt framed, dumped upon, his character called into question, his friends' ignorant judgments projected onto him—"for I know I am not what I am thought to be."[20]

Each degree of mounting pressure served to heighten the dilemma. Like Abraham earlier when asked to sacrifice Isaac, Job would not have been tried if he had known it was only a trial. If Job trusted God and suspended judgment, he had to be silent. But every moment he continued in silence was taken by others as a tacit admission that his friends were correct and he was guilty, which was outrageous. Yet to defend himself, he had to explain the suffering, which he couldn't. But to try to do so, he had to press reason to conclusions he had no desire to entertain and no right to make. This impossible situation was the torturous rack on which Job's faith was stretched to the breaking point. It is little wonder that his self-defense is a demonstration of faith mixed with doubt.

On the one hand, Job's faith reached heights of unrivaled courage, as when he cried, "But in my heart I know that my vindicator lives and that he will rise last to speak in court."[21] On the other hand, his chosen style of defense led him into the bitter blackness of self-pity and doubt, as wrong as it is understandable. In his reply, God rebuked Job for defending himself in a way that accused God: "Dare you deny that I am just or put me in the wrong that you may be right?"[22] In doing this, Job had dissolved the moral universe in one stroke and had brought down upon himself even more spiritual agony because he had made himself out to be more just than God.

What was the root of Job's mistake in not suspending judgment? Was it his blasphemy? No, that was only the result. At the root of his problem lay a fallacy in his thinking (the notion that he had enough information to make proper judgments in such a situation). Needless to say, Job's "fallacy" was more than intellectual. His sanctimonious comforters masked their envy, cruelty, and revulsion behind high-flying piety and "theologically correct" concerns. But like hens viciously attacking a wounded hen, they were rushing on him and attacking him with their sharp-beaked truth. And perhaps, as Simone Weil argues, their piously disguised hatred was beginning to penetrate to the center of Job's soul and poison his spirit. Weil writes, "If Job cries out that he is innocent in such despairing accents, it is because he himself is beginning not to believe in it, it is because his soul within him is beginning to take the side of his friends."[23]

But once Job defends himself by making conclusions he had no right to make, blasphemy was inevitable. So it is curious to see that both Job and his friends made a very similar mistake. Job's friends believed that God in his justice pays everyone his or her deserts *in this life.* Therefore they presupposed a one-to-one ratio between sin and suffering: Job was suffering; Job must have sinned.

Job roundly denies this. In their smug self-righteousness, his friends were terribly wrong and inexcusably cruel, as Pharisees—especially Christian Pharisees—always are. But in the absence of any explanation from God, he has no way to deny what they say. So in defending himself, he demands from God a one-to-one ratio between suffering and explanation, between pain and meaning. Thus both Job and his friends press reason too far and make judgments where they have no right to. The two errors lead in opposite directions, one toward cruelty and the other toward blasphemy, but they are both minted from the same coin.

Jeremiah shows us a different way altogether. Experiencing a personal crisis as the thrust of his ministry brought him deeper into misunderstanding, he cries, "He has broken my teeth on gravel; fed on ashes, I am wracked with pain; peace has gone out of my life."[24] But Jeremiah does not go on to judge God and demand an explanation. Instead he rests his case with God and suspends judgment for the moment. He adds, "The LORD, I say, is all that I have; therefore I will wait for him patiently."[25]

John Bunyan makes a similar point in *The Pilgrim's Progress* when Interpreter takes Christian and shows him a fire burning in a grate with a man standing in front of the fire flinging water on it. For some reason the fire does not go out but blazes higher and higher. Interpreter then takes Christian behind the wall and shows him the secret. A second man is secretly applying oil to the fire to counter the work of the man with the water. Seen from one side, nothing but water is put on the fire, but it still blazes higher because the oil is more effective than the water, even though it is secret.

Interpreter explains that the fire is a picture of the work of God in our lives. The man on the outside with the water (who is all that can be seen) represents the Devil, while the man with the oil can behind the wall represents the work of Christ in maintaining faith. Interpreter concludes, "And in that thou sawest that the man has stood behind the wall to maintain the fire, this is to teach thee that it is hard for the tempted to see how this work of grace is maintained in the soul."[26]

DO WE KNOW WHY?

There is one thing we must not skate over too quickly, or in our haste we may not notice that the ice is thin until too late. If suspended judgment turns on the principle "We do not know why, but we know why we trust God who knows why," it is all-important that we *do know why we trust God*. Of course, we say, I know why I trust him! but this can be the sort of easy self-assurance that wears threadbare after the first few moments of suffering.

We have no way of knowing how much strain our faith can take until we actually suffer. Only then do we know whether our faith is grounded where it should be. Very few of us pass the test of suffering well. When the chips are down and we do not know why we can trust God, we may find very soon that we do not see why we should. As I said, a full discussion of how we are able to trust God is beyond our concern here. What matters here is to show how significant trust in God can be in a time of suffering.

If all religious issues were boiled down to their essence, there would be two inescapable questions: Is God there? And, is God good? Our view of the existence of God and the character of God are the truths that determine all our other answers.

For Christians, the answer to both questions "How may I be sure that God is there and that God is good?" is answered satisfactorily only in Jesus Christ. Any "proof" of God's existence or argument in favor of his goodness that ends elsewhere is bound to be inconclusive or wrong. However cogent and compelling they may seem as arguments, in the long run they will prove both intellectually weak and emotionally unsatisfying, and there is nothing like suffering to show up this flaw.

The test of suffering reveals whether our "knowing why" is an irreducible bedrock conviction grounded in the revelation of God in Jesus Christ, or whether our faith is resting to any degree on what is not bedrock but sand. In this connection we can make two equal, though opposite mistakes, both of which end in making God so remote that we do not know why we can trust him in a time of suffering.

TOO FAR OFF FOR COMFORT

The first mistake is to identify Jesus so much with God the Father that we forget that God became human in Jesus and is one with us in our humanity. So there is no one who stands between God and humanity. The danger then is that God will become remote—in our feelings if not in our theology—and that in his remoteness his silence will be mistaken for his absence.

When we are in pain God's silence hurts. We suffer, we look up, we cry out, we pray, we tear our hearts out, but there is no answer. The heavens are brass, the gates are locked, the phone is busy, and in the ringing nothingness of silence we wonder if God was ever there. "Be not deaf to my cry," says the Psalmist, "lest, if thou answer me with silence, I become like those who go down to the abyss."[27] Or as Gerard Manley Hopkins put it in his *Last Sonnets*:

> *And my lament*
> *Is cries countless, cries like dead letters sent*
> *To dearest him that lives alas! away.*[28]

What is difficult enough for believers who know why they trust God is unbearable for believers who are uncertain or for nominal believers. No generation bears more eloquent testimony to this than our own. In his play *The Devil and the Good Lord* Jean Paul Sartre portrays Goetz, a butchering soldier-turned-saint who grows disillusioned by his spiritual ineffectiveness and God's silence. Eventually he wonders if his creed is true or whether it is only his own voice shouting out loud to cover God's silence. Finally he bursts out,

I prayed, I demanded a sign. I sent messages to Heaven, no reply. Heaven ignored my very name. Each minute I wonder what I could BE in the eyes of God. Now I know the answer: nothing. God does not see me, God does not hear me, God does not know me. You see this emptiness over our heads? That is God. You see this gap in the door? It is God. You see that hole in the ground? That is God again. Silence is God. Absence is God. God is the loneliness of man.[29]

This terrible cry of uncertainty that trails off into unbelief is echoed many times in modern drama and literature. Increasingly, especially after Auschwitz, the problem of justice in an evil world is approached from the moral position that declares the bystander to be guilty—and therefore indicts God as the eternal bystander. As Dostoyevsky's Ivan argues, "All the knowledge in the world is not worth a child's tears."[30]

But even these literary examples fade in comparison with the eyewitness descriptions of those who have faced the silence of God in real experience. One example is Nobel Laureate Elie Wiesel's account of Auschwitz in *Night*. A Hungarian-born Jew, Elie Wiesel was a survivor of both Auschwitz and Buchenwald, and his book is a searing account of a small boy encountering unmasked evil.

> Never shall I forget that night, the first night in camp, which has turned my life into one long night, seven times cursed and seven times sealed. . . . Never shall I forget those flames which consumed my faith forever. Never shall I forget that nocturnal silence which deprived me, for all eternity, of the desire to live. Never shall I forget those moments which murdered my God and my soul and turned my dream to dust. Never shall I forget these things, even if I am condemned to live as long as God Himself. Never.[31]

And what of the Christian? Are we different because our courage is greater or our theological explanations more nimble? Far from it. We too recoil from such a snake pit of evil. We feel the same pain, the same agony, the same questions, the same silence. We do not know why either, but (and here alone is the difference) we know why we trust God who knows why.

And how is this? Because of another Jew, a Jew not in his youth, but in his prime, not under compulsion but freely, who took on himself the full desolation of God's silence so that after suffering in our place he might restore us to his Father, that then we might be sure that God is there and God is good.

For the Christian, the cry of Jesus, "My God, my God, why hast thou forsaken me?"[32] will always have depths of meaning that the human mind can never fathom. But one thing at least it means. None of us can sink so low that God has not gone lower still. As C. S. Lewis puts it, "Sometimes it is hard not to say 'God forgive God.' Sometimes it is hard to say so much. But if our faith is true, He didn't. He crucified him."[33]

Martin Luther once read the story of Abraham's sacrifice of Isaac in his family devotions. When he had finished his wife Katie said simply, "I do not believe it. God would not have treated his son like that."

"But, Katie," Luther answered, "he did."[34]

This is how doubts about the Father are silenced in the Son. God may become remote to us in times of suffering—unless he is "the God and Father of our Lord Jesus Christ." Do you catch the intimacy in that little give-away description of God? Jesus was known and loved by the disciples. To them he was *our* Lord Jesus Christ. They had followed him, lived with him, learned from him. They loved him, and they would lay down their lives for him. But who was God whom they had never seen? Quite simply he was "Jesus Christ's Father," and so they called him "the God, and Father of our Lord Jesus Christ." Didn't Jesus himself say, "Go to my brothers, and tell them that I am now ascending to my Father and your Father, my God and your God"?[35] Hadn't he taught them to pray "Our Father in heaven"?[36]

So the truth of the Incarnation is not just good theology; it is practical comfort and assurance. Jesus identifies with us in our humanity, and now we know that God is for us in Christ. The resistance leader can be trusted. He went through torture too. When we see Jesus on the cross we can come to trust God with an unutterable trust that never for a moment considers he will not stand by us in our sufferings. Dostoyevsky was so passionate about Christ that he asserted that, if there were any contradiction, he would choose Christ rather than truth. Much of this passion went back to an experience of being profoundly moved by the suffering of Christ as he stood in front of Holbein's painting, "Descent from the Cross."

> I know that the Christian Church laid it down, even in the early ages, that Christ's suffering was not symbolical but actual, and that His body on the cross was therefore fully and completely subject to the laws of nature. In the picture the face is fearfully crushed by blows, swollen, covered by fearful, swollen and blood-stained bruises, the eyes are open and squinting: the great, wide-open whites of the eyes glitter with a sort of deathly, glassy light.[37]

To Dostoyevsky, Holbein's painting was more than graphic realism. It portrayed the reality of the universe. There could be redemption in the world if God's son had suffered like this. As Dostoyevsky acknowledged at the very end of his life: He had come to God through Christ having gone through "the hell-fire of doubt."[38]

TOO CLOSE FOR COMFORT

This emphasis on Christ's suffering, however, can lead easily to the opposite mistake—to see Jesus as so much one with our humanity that we forget that in his deity he is still one with God the Father. We may identify him so completely with ourselves that he is not the Father's volunteer but God's victim whose death is a meaningless sacrifice.

As this extreme sees it, Christ has become one with us, so in his greater suffering there is comfort to all lesser suffering, but the comfort is meager and short-lived. Its value is relative and not absolute, for it has achieved nothing finally. God the Father is still angry and implacable or distant and remote. So Christ's death is a magnificent statement, a heroic gesture, an inspiring symbol, but it is essentially tragic, wasted, and futile. After all, if he is not God, why should the death of one Jew be different from the death of six million other Jews?

Arthur Koestler's dramatic soliloquy "The Misunderstanding" is a typical modern expression of this mistake. It pictures Christ on the road to Calvary, carrying his cross painfully and issuing a challenge to God to look down from heaven and care or to look away forever:

> Are you the one who is playing these games with Adam's seed? Or are you only absent-minded and asleep? Soon I shall know when this stake and I change places, when instead of me carrying it, it will carry me. That will be the test, your trial. Then I shall know.
>
> If that is the case and you are only distracted or asleep, I shall pull your sleeve in my pain until you wake up and my purpose is achieved. But if you are that deaf and dumb spirit, then pulling your sleeve will be a gesture of a fool, and dying will be hard.[39]

Is the cross just a vicious trap into which Jesus was led by God? Is it only a bad joke played on him by an indifferent deity? Is it merely a travesty of justice so extreme that protest and revolution will never want for a hero? Is Jesus God only because he is the poorest and most suffering of men? These are questions that clamor for our attention if we make this second mistake. And it is obvious that, though dramatically opposed, the result is still the same. God is still remote and his silence, which this time is silence to Christ as well as ourselves, is taken as proof of his absence.

This extreme, like the other, depends on a caricature of Christ. It emphasizes only a half-truth. In contrast, the Bible, which spares nothing in stressing Christ's identification with us as human beings, does not stop there. Jesus freely became human for a purpose—a purpose that cost God the Father as much as it did God the Son, a purpose that was successfully carried out and vindicated by the resurrection. Not surprisingly those whose faith in God is anchored in the Incarnation—God become flesh, crucified, risen—can pass through the fires of suffering. For there is no question however deep or painful that cannot be trusted with the God who is the Father of Jesus Christ.

Trusting God with our questions is true not only of questions raised by suffering but of all our questions that are unanswerable in this life, questions that tax the power of speculation and push it beyond its limits and so raise anxiety for faith. (For example, Why did God create if he knew that . . . ?) These are different from nonsense questions, which are unanswerable in a different sense. (C. S. Lewis wrote, "All nonsense questions are unanswerable. How many hours are in a mile? Is yellow square or round? Probably half the questions we ask—half our great theological and metaphysical problems—are like that."[40]) Nonsense questions will never be answerable, even by God. But these pain-triggered questions are only unanswerable to us in this life. There are facts of life in a fallen world that we will never be able to explain but must never explain away. Faith, however, can suspend judgment on these questions, for there is no question we cannot leave with God if he is the Father of Jesus Christ.

GETTING EVEN WITH GOD

The special temptation to doubt in suffering comes from the fact that we feel someone should answer for the suffering, but no one is answerable. So we are left, it seems, with one of two choices. Either we must find the answer within ourselves, by resigning ourselves to it or condemning ourselves for it. Or else we must answer back by accusing, or at least questioning, someone else. It is difficult to hold an impersonal universe personally responsible, and nothing less than personal responsibility will finally do. The only remaining option is to call God to the bar and charge him with the injustice of suffering that is otherwise inexplicable. Through doubt we can get even with God.

Have you ever noticed how people who emphatically deny that God is there are often the first to assert that he is not good? "Why does God allow . . . ?" can be an atheist's theoretical question designed to challenge the credibility of faith. But just as often it can be an atheist's passionate personal challenge to the irrationality of suffering. If God is allowed to be personal nowhere else, he must be personal here. In this sense, blame is a useful index of belief, for everyone believes in God at least as much as he or she blames God for suffering that cannot be explained in any other way.

The same is true of us as believers too. If suffering without explanation creates doubt, doubt is a makeshift explanation for suffering. If we are hurting and can get no answer from God, the best way to get back at God is to doubt his goodness. We then have a picture of God at which we can throw the blame. Doubt becomes a counterfeit answer to suffering, for if God is like that, he is to blame. Now at least one of the questions raised by suffering is crossed off our list.

It is always easier to hurt most those we know best. In the

same way, there is nothing like doubt to gather up and throw back the bitterness faith feels when it is left in the lurch by unexplained suffering. Reflecting on his own dark thoughts after his bereavement, C. S. Lewis admitted, "All that stuff about the cosmic sadist was not so much the expression of thought as of hatred. I was getting from it the only pleasure a man in anguish can get; the pleasure of hitting back."[41]

If there is just one person we can blame, and if we can do this in any way at all, even in the most unconscious and hidden of grudges, then there is at least some shelter from the heat of the questions raised by apparently meaningless suffering. But if we suffer and there is absolutely no one to blame, we are stranded like someone naked on the fiery anvil of the desert sands before the sun at high noon. Little wonder that faith is sorely tempted to curse God and die.

A thousand years earlier than Lewis, Peter Abelard acknowledged how unfair he had been to blame God for the monstrous evils people had done to him, including castration. "God who judges equity, with what bitterness of spirit and anguish of mind did I reproach you in my madness and accuse you in my fury, constantly repeating the lament of St. Antony, 'Good Jesus, where were you?' All the grief and indignation, the blushes for shame, the agony of despair I suffered, I cannot put into words."[42]

FAITH IS NOT REPRESSION

Suspending judgment is often like walking in the dark along a narrow path with a steep cliff on either side. If there are dangers on the side of answering back, there are also dangers on the side of not answering back. The danger here is that in suspending judgment we go on to deny the emotional reality of our experience and turn faith into repression.

To suspend judgment on *why* something is happening is not the same as denying *that* something is happening. The former is faith, the latter is repression, which should have no part in the Christian faith. It is not the business of faith to deny reality but to order it. Denying reality is a mark of make-believe, not of living faith. The sort of faith that needs the protective gloves of evasion and euphemism condemns itself to a timid, sickly existence. Such faith is a pale and delicate imitation of true faith, a counterfeit that encourages hypocrisy and heartlessness in the name of surface appearances and the niceness of orthodoxy.

Biblical faith, in contrast, is full-blooded and down-to-earth. Look at Jesus and you see God's face wet with human tears and God's heart roused with outrage. To trust God did not mean for Jesus the denial of the evil and brokenness of the world but the absolute refusal to make it determinative. The temptation to deny reality is the Devil's clever attempt to turn suspended judgment inside out. It goes through the same motions and makes the same gestures but achieves the opposite result. To deny reality does not answer the problems raised by reality; it only affirms that they are insuperable to faith and insists that they remain so.

There are many elements of repression in contemporary faith. What we saw earlier in relation to doubt is equally true of Christian attitudes toward other emotions, such as feelings of failure, depression, or grief. Over much of the stiff, tight-corseted unnaturalness that poses as Christian faith we might engrave the sound advice of Shakespeare:

> *What man, ne'er pull your hat upon your brows.*
> *Give sorrow words; the grief that does not speak*
> *Whispers the o'er-fraught heart, and bids it break.*[43]

Augustine demonstrated the honesty and freedom of a better way. Writing after his mother's death, he admitted, "The tears which I had been holding back streamed down, and I let them flow as freely as they would, making of them a pillow for my heart. On them it rested, for my weeping sounded in your ears alone."[44] He owed to his mother not only his physical birth but his spiritual birth too, and at her death he was not ashamed to express his profound grief.

One of the ways faith is turned into repression is by distorted teaching—for example, when faith is turned into faith-in-faith rather than faith-in-God, or when thanksgiving is misdirected and strains for a praise that is unnatural. At first sight, the emphasis on praise and thanksgiving is so welcome that it seems churlish to question it. But when the biblical injunction to "give thanks whatever happens"[45] is taught with wooden literalism, it not only contradicts much of the Bible, it can also be psychologically damaging. Yet Christians are sometimes counseled today to praise God even for evil.

This is a dangerous travesty of biblical teaching. Jesus did not give God thanks for everything. Face to face with evil, Jesus was outraged; face to face with suffering and sin, he wept. And if it were not for that anger and those tears and the resolute road to the cross that they marked, we would not realize how outraged by evil God is and how seriously he takes sin. The dilemma is not the result of tension between the biblical view of things and our experience of things, as if faith were opposed to reality. The dilemma comes from the tension between the biblical view of evil (a reality God hates and is not to be thanked for) and the biblical call for us to trust God and give him thanks whatever happens.

AS HUMAN AS GOD MADE US

One way out of the perplexity is to isolate our experiences in life, and think of them in terms of their overall character and the components that make them up. When an experience is considered in terms of its overall character, our appropriate response to God is unreserved trust and thanksgiving. There is no situation so evil that it is beyond redeeming by God. From this perspective, it is always right to trust God and give thanks. Jeremiah expresses this sense of trust in God's sovereignty even over evil when he says,

> Who can command and it is done,
>   if the LORD has forbidden it?
> Do not both bad and good proceed
>   from the mouth of the Most High? . . .
> let us lift up our hearts, not our hands,
>   to God in heaven.[46]

But if we think of the same experience in terms of its components, it may well include things that are evil, painful, and disappointing or, as the case may be, good, beneficial, and delightful. We can respond appropriately to each of these individual elements, and in many instances our response should not be thanks. Outrage is appropriate in response to genuine wrong, tears in response to grief, shock in response to unexpected disaster. We mustn't force ourselves to thank God *for these things* or we will be harder on ourselves and softer on evil than God is. It is not that *even* Christians need not give thanks for these things, but that Christians *especially* should not give thanks for them. We should always be as human as God made us.

The balance of faith and realism is as true to Scripture as it is comforting to us. Augustine, as if anticipating this sort of distorted teaching, wrote, "Who would wish for hardship and difficulty? You command us to endure these troubles, not to love them. No one loves what he endures even though he may be glad to endure it."[47] Martin Luther puts it equally strongly:

"God has not created man to be a stock or stone but has given him five senses and a heart of flesh, so that he loves his friends, is angry with his enemies, and commiserates with his dear friends in adversity."[48]

If God has made us this way, will he ask us to live in a way that is unnatural to the way in which he has created us? If he has made us capable of the full range of human emotions, are we to bottle them up in practice? We can be sure that he will never forget our humanness, and we should do no less with ourselves.

One of the wonders of Christian faith in time of suffering is its humanness. Where Muslims resign themselves, Buddhists and Hindus withdraw, stoics endure, and existentialists fight in vain, the Christian can exult. But the fierce joy of Christian exultation is not triumphalism. Nor is it superficial. We exult because in knowing God we know the outcome, but this is no protection from the pain of suffering in between. "We are tossed on a tide that puts us to the proof," wrote Augustine, "and if we could not sob our troubles in your ear, what hope should we have left to us?"[49] Or as Fyodor Dostoyevsky wrote of his pain-fired faith, "It is not as a boy that I believe in Christ and confess him, but my hosanna has passed through a great furnace of doubts."[50]

> I remain loyal to His Name although every common-sense fact gives the lie to Him, and declares that He has no more power than a morning mist.
>
> —Oswald Chambers

> It's a painful thing to be misjudged. But it's no more than God puts up with every hour of the day. But he is patient. So long as He knows he's in the right, He lets folk think what they like—'til He has time to make them know better. Lord, make my heart clean within me, and then I'll care little for any judgment but yours![51]
>
> —George Macdonald

—————■▌—————

CHAPTER 11

HOW LONG, O LORD?

Doubt from Impatience

Some years ago I was waiting in the emergency room of a busy London hospital. Casualties seemed to pour in from all sides, but there seemed to be no matching urgency. I was struck by the change in the way people waited. Those who were alert and eager, almost impatient, were those who had arrived most recently. They sat up every time a name was called out, expecting it to be theirs. But gradually they became like the rest who had been there longer. Resigned, staring blankly, those who had been there longest sometimes even missed their names when they were eventually called.

It is never easy to wait, because waiting does something to us. Waiting also tells us something. It shows what our relationship is to the person or the event we are waiting for. Would a man wait for his fiancée in the way he waits for his income tax bill? If he did, it might not tell us much about his fiancée, but it would tell us volumes about his opinion of her. Some people can keep us waiting for hours and we don't mind. But if others are only a minute or two late we get impatient. Why should she keep *me* waiting? In short, waiting shows us what we think of the person who keeps us waiting.

The second of the two torturing questions is like this, for the question "How long, O Lord?" turns into the doubt, *Who does God think he is to keep us waiting?* This doubt comes when a particular vision God has given us seems utterly impossible or hopelessly delayed. The hardest thing to do then is to wait and work on. Waiting does something to us, and it tells us something about our relationship to God. The lesson of this last doubt is that suspending judgment does not mean suspending operations. As Martin Luther wrote, "There is a big difference between suffering injustice and keeping still. We should suffer. We should not keep still."[1]

This doubt and the previous one are closely related. The ability to suspend judgment and the ability to wait and work on are basic skills of faith. Each is an art that presupposes and complements the other, and both are automatically challenged whenever faith is challenged, though in different ways. In suspending judgment, faith stays true to God by not doing what it is tempted to do, whereas in waiting and working on faith stays true to God by doing what it is tempted not to. The two doubts are different sides of the same coin, and they are both extremely difficult. In refusing to suspend judgment, we may lose hold of God's character; in refusing to wait, we lose sight of our own calling.

EVERY CHRISTIAN A VISIONARY

Every Christian should be a visionary. When we come to know God, the illumination of his truth breaks into every part of life. Our worldview is changed and our sense of calling is wholly transformed. But vision is more than this. Its key idea is not operation (the essence of a worldview) but inspiration, or operation raised to the level of inspiration.

Commitment to God is commitment to God's vision of things, so Christian vision is a Christian view of the world that has caught fire and is ablaze with the knowledge of God. God's character and God's calling transcend the immediacy of seen reality, reinterpret the entire picture of our immediate lives, and call us to realities that are beyond and above. This is the vision of faith, insight that leads to through-sight, so that in all circumstances, despite all appearances, what is seen through the finite and the visible is the eternal and the invisible.

This vision of faith takes the flow of time and history and charges them with a dynamic of hope, freeing the Christian to wait for God with meaning. If time were only cyclical, a process of infinite change, it would quite literally be going nowhere. Life's highest goal would be as the Hindus and Buddhists see it—detachment, not involvement. The pursuit of purpose within time would be eternally thwarted and futile. On the other hand, if time were only linear, a mere sequence of moments, either human beings would have to conquer time and impose their meaning on it or time conquers human beings. Like a jailer, it would hurry humanity down the corridor of the years to the death sentence that awaits it at the end.

But the Christian view of time is different from either, not because our experience of time is different but because our evaluation of time is transformed by the vision of God's truth. Seeing this, faith is able to bring together both the vision and the vehicle by which it is achieved, so that the means of faith and the end of faith form an unbroken link. Faith not only sees, it substantiates what it sees. It is concerned with the reality beyond and with making it real here and now. As the celebrated passage in Hebrews begins, "Faith gives substance to our hopes, and makes us certain of realities we do not see."[2]

Oswald Chambers captures this characteristic dynamism of faith. "It is not what a man achieves, but what he believes and strives for that makes him noble and great. . . . There is a difference between a perfect human life lived on earth and a personal life with God lived on earth; the former grasps for that which it reaches, the latter is grasped by that which it can never reach. The former chains us to earth by its very completeness; the latter causes us to fling ourselves unperplexed on God."[3]

This means there is a creative tension within Christian faith. The Hebrew word for faith has the same stem as the word for hope, and the root meaning of both is tautness or tension. As Thomas Brooks, the seventeenth-century Puritan, wrote, "Waiting is indeed but an act of faith further stretched out."[4] Faith that lacks this stretchedness is less than it should be. The Christian view of things is pitted ultimately against the vision of other faiths and worldviews. It stands over against every perception of reality that is finite from end to end. Faith sees the infinite as well as the finite or it sees nothing. The tension of faith results from its being stretched between God's promise and God's fulfillment, and if one or other of these is thought to fail, the line of faith sags or snaps.

Faith's calling is to live in between times. Faith is in transit. It lives in an interim period. Behind faith is the great "no longer." Ahead of it lies the great "not yet." God has spoken and God will act. Christ has come once and Christ will come again. We have heard the promises and we will witness the event. However long the waiting takes, it is only the gap between the thunder and the lightning.

Faith's task is to join hands with the past and the future to hold down God's will in the present. The present moment is the disputed territory for faith, a no-man's-land between past and future, ground either to be seized by obedience or lost to disobedience. Visionary faith stakes out its possession of the land and does so with energy and enthusiasm that come from its knowledge of what the reclaimed land will one day be.

Picture in your mind a couple walking through a bare, unfurnished house. What makes them so excited and keen to buy it? It isn't what they see but what they see in what they see. Being creative and full of ideas, they see what it might be where others see only what it is. The vision of faith is like this. It has ideas about the future that are God's ideas. God himself is the one who "summons things that are not yet in existence as if they already were."[5] Vision is not a matter of seeing what is and asking why. It is far more a matter of seeing what has never yet been and asking why not.

Are you a visionary? Is your Christian faith merely functional and routine, or does it inspire you, throwing light and meaning on all you do, moving ahead of you like a pillar of cloud and fire? We are called to be down-to-earth as Christians but not to be earthbound.

THE DEFENSE NEVER RESTS

Hebrews 11 is the great Honors List of visionary faith, a stirring catalogue of men and women whose vision of God called them to live and work over against the customs, values, and priorities of their generation. They marched to a different drummer. Their sights were on a different goal. Their home was in a different country. They looked forward to a different city. By their faith, they called the entire world in question, and Hebrews says of them, "Those who use such language show plainly that they are looking for a country of their own."[6]

The secret of visionary faith lies in that sentence. How is it that they managed to transcend their times, surmounting the immediate, living over against the generally accepted, looking beyond the impossible? They were not an elite. The secret is simply that their whole lives were speaking and acting with the language and logic of the alternative vision that is proper to faith.

The language and the logic of visionary faith is a demanding style of argument. It is easy enough to understand but difficult to substantiate, for once it is stated it can be substantiated only in life. So those who are not prepared to back their words with their lives will find that their use of the argument will be too costly or quite ineffective.

This style of argument is illustrated in *Strong Poison,* an early novel of Dorothy Sayers. The story opens with Harriet Vane in the dock, on trial for the murder of a writer with whom she had been living. There is a strong, apparently watertight case against her. The prosecution, who do not know her personally, are pressing for a verdict of guilty. Undeniably she had the motivation and the opportunity. All the known facts of the case are against her. She should hang.

But into the grave situation steps the hero, Lord Peter Wimsey. He believes in her innocence and therefore he is sure that, although the known facts are against her, the known facts are not all the facts. So what he does is set out to discover and demonstrate the missing facts that would change the picture completely. Lord Peter argues with his colleagues, "There must be evidence somewhere, you know. I know you have all worked like beavers, but I am going to work like a king beaver. And I've got one big advantage over the rest of you . . . I do believe in Miss Vane's innocence."[7]

This is exactly the argument used by visionary faith. Followers of Christ know why they trust that God is there and that God is good. In accepting the consequences of this knowledge, they rise to a life-calling that sets them against the grain of the contemporary social reality and tests to the limits the obedience of their faith. Time and again they believe God and are prepared to obey even though it does not visibly pay or work. Other options repeatedly seem easier. Worse still, they sometimes seem more natural, more logical, even more right than God's way.

At such times are believers to trust God and so maintain the tension of faith in the face of pressure? Or are they to bow to the current odds and, in trying to ease the strain on faith, destroy the tension altogether, replacing faith with doubt? This is the challenge to visionaries, and their reply is audacious. Knowing why they trust God, they trust and wait. The *known* facts are against God, but the known facts are not *all* the facts.

DIDN'T I TELL YOU?

Lord Peter Wimsey's defense highlights two things that are important to this style of argument. First, it does not matter how overwhelming the case appears to be so long as we know why the accused is innocent. If we are unsure of this, the whole argument collapses. We could never be sure that the known facts of the case were *not* all the facts, and any arguments to counter the apparently watertight case against the accused might sound no stronger than wishful thinking.

But this is what we have underlined about faith in God all along. If there is "no reason why" when faith is present, there will certainly be "no reason why not" when doubt arrives. If we say that we trust God, there is no virtue in siding with him *in the end*, belatedly hurrying forward, as it were, to congratulate God when the verdict is given in his favor. Knowing why we can trust God, we should be loyal friends who believe in his integrity *all along*. The final vindication adds nothing to faith except the chance to turn round and say to doubt, "Didn't I tell you?" Oswald Chambers expresses it baldly: "Unless we can look the darkest, blackest fact full in the face without damaging God's character, we do not yet know Him."[8]

The second point is equally simple. Lord Peter's line of

defense needed substantiating. Merely to state it might have meant an interesting headline ("PEER SPEAKS UP FOR MURDER-ESS"), but it would not have cleared Harriet Vane of the charge. It is the same with faith. Without obedience, faith is no more than an interesting theoretical statement. To become credible it must be "real"-ized in practice. This is the point of saying that even when the vision is delayed, faith must wait and work on. There is a form of waiting that is an act of faith, and another which is an act of laziness, carelessness, or despair. Only the former is related to the obedience of faith.

This style of argument is common in the Bible, and there are striking illustrations of it that are just as telling as those in Hebrews 11. One is the Old Testament belief in the physical resurrection of believers, despite the fact that this had neither a solid precedent in history nor a full theological explanation until the resurrection of Jesus centuries later. This belief was not wishful thinking, a romantic sidestepping. The Hebrews were blunt and frank about death.

All known facts pointed to one conclusion: Death is the end. "But remember this: wise men must die; stupid men, brutish men, all perish. . . . For men are like oxen whose life cannot last."[9] If, however, there is an undying value to the person who is made in God's image and who trusts God, then the known facts were obviously not all the facts, and Isaiah could say:

> But thy dead live, their bodies will rise again.
>   They that sleep in the earth will awake and shout for joy;
> for thy dew is a dew of sparkling light,
>   and the earth will bring those long dead to birth again.[10]

Another remarkable example of this style of argument can be found in Jeremiah's prayer to God during the siege of Jerusalem. It was the tenth year of the reign of King Zedekiah over Judah. Jerusalem was in the merciless grip of the Babylonian siege. Jeremiah himself was in prison, and God had just informed him of the imminent fall of the city. On every hand the outlook and prospects were bleak. No time must have seemed less suitable for long-range planning, let alone confident business enterprises. But this was the exact moment when God told Jeremiah that his cousin would come and offer to sell him the family land and that he was to buy it.

If Jeremiah had not known why he trusted God, an order like this would have sounded ludicrous, unreal, completely out of touch with the facts of the situation. If ever there was a time not to buy and sell property, it was then. But when his cousin came, Jeremiah obeyed God and bought the land. The known facts of the situation were all against it, but if God had told him to do it, then clearly the known facts were not all the facts and do it he must. By his act of obeying God he argued with appearances and defied the obvious, and his perplexity is evident in his prayer:

> Look at the siege-ramps, the men who are advancing to take the city, and the city given over to its assailants from Chaldaea, the victim of sword, famine, and pestilence. The word thou hast spoken is fulfilled and thou dost see it. And yet thou hast bidden me buy the field, O LORD God and have the deed witnessed, even though the city is given to the Chaldaeans.[11]

This is faith's characteristic style. God's word is normative and all else is judged by it. The waters may be dark and swirling, but faith steps from one stepping stone of God's Word to another. Visibility may be poor, but faith pursues the vision from one glimpse to another, undeterred by whatever stands across its path. If God says so, God must know why. Then the argument is not with God but with the contradictions of the situation that deny his lordship.

So Noah listened to God and built an ark. So Abraham left home and country and lived in a tent, waiting for a more permanent city. So Sarah conceived a child though she was well past the age. So Moses crossed the Red Sea as if it was dry land. And the letter to the Hebrews comments, "They were not yet in possession of the things promised, but had seen them far ahead and hailed them. . . . That is why God is not ashamed to be called their God."[12]

THE STIFFEST TEST

But, and this after all is the point, this style of argument is extremely demanding. Not only does it provide no insurance against doubt, it increases the risk. There is always the possibility that the tension may be stretched to the breaking point. So Noah, who built the ark by faith, also fell into a drunken stupor. So Abraham, who trusted God with the life of his son, would not trust him with the safety of his wife. Most of the heroes of faith knew defeats like these.

What would you say is the hardest test for visionary faith— crisis, disappointment, disaster, or delay? Unquestionably it is delay. Nothing is harder for faith than waiting. That may sound surprising. Surely there is nothing easier to do than wait? Can't any old lazybones do that? True, there are forms of waiting that involve no effort at all. They are simply a matter of hanging around. But that is not the kind of waiting required in visionary faith. Because it is visionary, it can see more than is yet substantiated; because it is faith, it can wait for it. But being visionary faith, it is out to substantiate all that it has seen, so it can hardly wait for it.

Crisis and failure are much less painful to the vision of

faith than waiting. In fact they are important only because they involve waiting. If I remove the word *crisis* and substitute the word *setback* instead, you will see at once why a crisis is a problem for vision. It sets back the vision, and every postponement means even more waiting. Do you know people who say they have no problem with waiting for their vision? They might ask themselves if they have a vision worth waiting for. Equanimity can be a sign of indifference as much as faith. A sure mark of Christian vision is its godly impatience and holy restlessness.

Just as a plane presses at the sound barrier and shudders with the impact as it breaks through, the visionary through-sight of faith takes on itself the crushing weight of the contradictions of reality. Often there is a moment just prior to breakthrough when the pressure is most intense and faith seems to shudder with the strain, threatening even to disintegrate. This strain is what causes doubt. The immense weight of contradictory reality crashes against faith like a shockwave so that momentarily the clarity and single mindedness of the vision is lost and faith is thrown off course into a dazed state of double vision.

If this was true of those heroes of faith whom Hebrews describes by name, could it have been any different for those unnamed ones who were "tortured to death, disdaining release, to win a better resurrection"? Or of those who had to "face jeers and flogging, even fetters and prison bars. They were stoned, they were sawn in two, they were put to the sword, they went about dressed in skins of sheep or goats, in poverty, distress, and misery."[13] Do we imagine that they were never in two minds? Do we believe they had no second thoughts?

Jesus is the pioneer of visionary faith. "For the sake of the joy that lay ahead of him, [he] endured the cross, making light of its disgrace."[14] Yet even he experienced anguish of spirit as his obedience to God's will put him at odds with the will of the world. Looking into the horror of the cross, he cried out, "Now my soul is in turmoil, and what am I to say? Father, save me from this hour. No, it was for this that I came to this hour."[15]

And when Jesus' cry of abandonment rang out from the cross itself, we may remind ourselves that he was quoting and fulfilling the Old Testament, we may reassure ourselves that it was not a cry of despair but a prayer to God, we may rejoice that its sequel was the cry of triumph, "It is finished." But we must never be so blinded by sentiment that we minimize the horror, the alienation, and the bitterness of that hour. There, if ever, Jesus must have been tempted to doubt.

Don't be fooled by the strenuous language of the last few pages. Curiously, waiting is especially hard for activists— which is a type of character our modern world encourages. Lacking a balance between action and contemplation, and emphasizing masculine characteristics at the expense of the feminine, activists are highly regarded today, whether men or women. Energetic, ambitious, restless, rational, calculating, they manage themselves, other people, and life itself. But underneath their obvious "leadership" and "success," their activism has a dubious quality. They find their identity in doing and having, not in being. And it is exactly this frenzied drivenness that is stopped dead by waiting. Just *being* is disconcerting to those who must always be *doing*.

Goethe's Faust was an insatiable seeker and an unbridled activist. And it is no accident that in his contract with the devil he curses not only faith, hope, and love but the quality needed for waiting: "And cursed be Patience most of all."[16]

Waiting in faith is not easy. It is one thing to be fired by a vision and get up out of an armchair. It is another to be fired by a vision and walk through fire and rain. It is one thing to be stirred by the reminder that every crisis is an opportunity to demonstrate faith. It is another to translate the vision into reality and to pay the price of doing so. And never to give up even when everything's stalled. Yet for visionary faith only the latter counts.

STIMULATED OR STYMIED?

The book of Revelation looks forward to a time when "there shall be no more delay . . . the hidden purpose of God will have been fulfilled."[17] But that day is still in the great "not yet" for us, and until it dawns every exultant "Hallelujah!" will sooner or later be followed on the Christian's lips by an impassioned "How long, O Lord?" The latter expresses the unique pain and distress as the vision of God is thwarted or denied by the reality of a world in rebellion.

"Our trust in God will be perfect," wrote Martin Luther, "when life and death, glory and shame, adversity and prosperity, will be the same to us."[18] But that is another way of saying that our trust in God will never be perfect in this life. In this life, the only alternative to the inevitable ups and downs of human experience is not perfection but the zombie-like trance of total detachment. Perfection is impossible, detachment is wrong. So as long as we live, we will know the ups and downs, and their challenge to faith will be the same double option we have seen all along: Will each crisis stimulate or stymie faith?

Speaking of a robust faith, Pascal says, "There is some pleasure in being on board a ship battered by storms when one is certain of not perishing. The persecutions buffeting the Church are like this."[19] But what is true of the church in persecution is not always true of the individual Christian in time of doubt. Doubt is lonelier than persecution.

A better test for faith is to catch it off guard in a time of failure, upset, or delay, and watch its reactions then. The off-duty reaction is the one that shows the caliber of faith. "Though he slay me, yet will I trust in him"[20] is both credible and proper when Job says it, because he had almost been slain and he was still trusting. But it is quite another matter for people to say it if they never expect God to slay them and have made very sure that the possibility is unlikely to arise.

The corrosion of waiting eats first into the sense of total involvement with our work. We are forced to stand back and think about it rather than do it. Waiting eats next into the time-tables we have set for ourselves, delaying them, setting them back, making us wonder if they are feasible or if they are worth it. Soon it is eating into the worthwhileness of what we are doing. If it cannot be done as we originally intended or if it looks as if it will never be finished, is it worth doing at all?

Before long the corrosion eats into our souls and we ourselves are called in question. Will we ever finish the work God has given us? Has God shown us what he wants us to do next and we've missed it? Will he ever show us? Perhaps we are unready? Perhaps we will never be ready? Perhaps we are useless to God?

No wonder it seems easiest to stop waiting. This puts a stop to faith and necessitates doubt, but at least it stops the torture of waiting. Whether we act in panic or impatience, at least we have the satisfaction of taking things into our own hands. It may even release us from the temptation to blame God. One moment longer and we might be saying, "Who does God think he is to keep us waiting?"

The agonizing wait stretches a believer on a rack. If we maintain faith, we feel tortured even more and no one seems to come to our rescue. All that is wanted, our torturer says, is that we recant and deny that anyone will come to our aid. Our faith as believers is then caught: Heads-I-win, tails-you-lose. If we maintain faith, there seems to be no guarantee that our rescuer will come to our aid, and our situation is torture only because we do maintain faith. On the other hand, if we recant, we will be free and we will be our own rescuer. So the choice is flattering. This is the way doubt reasons with faith under the trial of waiting, and if faith gives in, its recanting is doubt.

PREVENTION AND CURE

What is the preventative for this doubt? First, we must check the vision behind it. Only a genuine vision can be expected to come true. History is strewn with the ruins of follies that were the result of private lines to God. Is the vision from God himself? Is it in accord with the rest of God's revelation of himself? How much of selfish and impure motivations are mixed in and need to be purified first? When the testing comes it may be too late to answer these questions. Better to ask them before and be sure of the answers.

Of course a vision will fail if it is false. It may also fail because it is not practiced as it should be. One pale version of visionary faith is the talk of hope that preoccupies itself with an object of hope (such as the second coming of Jesus) but never expresses that hope in action. Without something to hope for, we are literally hope-less. Without a reason to hope for it, we are only hoping against hope. But even with the best object and the best reason in the world hope is still not fully Christian unless it issues in a dynamic of living that demonstrates the hope in action.

One counterfeit of visionary faith is the comfortable idea that waiting is only a matter of waiting in situations where, humanly speaking, we have to wait anyway. Thus some people wait only when it is impossible to do anything else. But this removes the dimension of faith from waiting and reduces it to resignation. Activism and resignation are equally a denial of faith in God, though in different ways. It is not so hard to wait when we have to, when everyone else is waiting too. But can we trust God and wait when everyone else is moving on, going somewhere, doing something? Or must we take things into our own hands, decide for ourselves, and make the best move we can? That is the test.

Second, it is important to feed and exercise faith. Seeing a vision is like being born, a once-for-all experience. But maintaining the vision is like growing; it needs daily nourishment. The stiffer the test the better faith's diet must be and the more strenuous its exercise. The more tension faith faces in some areas, the more relaxation and refreshment it needs in others. The more it is opposed by the powers of this world, the more it must experience the powers of the age to come. Waiting for God is absolutely dependent on waiting on God.

A comparison of two biblical incidents shows the possibilities clearly. The first occurred during the ministry of the prophet Elisha when Samaria, the capital of the northern kingdom of Israel, was under siege by Benhadad, King of Syria. When the situation became desperate the King of Israel cried out, "Look at our plight! This is the LORD's doing. Why should I wait any longer for him to help us?"[21] Once his ordinary human endurance had run out, he could wait no longer since he had no faith. But if it was God's doing, as he said it was, then to refuse to wait for God was illogical. Yet the reaction was human. Waiting was so intolerable that something had to be done to break the hopelessness of waiting. In taking things into his own hands, he demonstrated that waiting was showing up his lack of faith.

The second incident took place in an equally grave situation as the southern kingdom of Judah was attacked during the ministry of Isaiah in the ninth century B.C. King and people were shaken like trees in the wind, but Isaiah took his stand against the mounting panic and the repeated attempts to find help apart from God. "Have firm faith, or you will not stand firm," he says.[22] Or as he expanded on this later, "Come back, keep peace, and you will be safe; in stillness and in staying quiet, there lies your strength."[23]

Isaiah is the prophet of faith. When he condemns Judah, it is not for its wickedness alone, but for its shortsighted reliance on untrustworthy gods. Each crisis sends the people reeling in fresh panic and shows that their trust was not in God in the first place. In contrast, Isaiah was the living example of his own teaching. If faith is a radical reliance on God, it is undaunted by circumstances, unaltered by the odds. Even when it faces what is humanly impossible, faith can still stand at full stretch. Such faith is the antithesis of self-reliant humanism. When the strongest self-reliance has broken down, such faith will still be standing.

Isaiah's supreme expression of this is in chapter 40. Appropriately it follows from the awesome vision of God's character and power. Other faiths may fall short, other people in their prime may grow weary, "but those who look to the LORD will win new strength, they will grow wings like eagles; they will run and not be weary, they will march on and never grow faint."[24]

Faith that waits is not resigned. Nor is it hoping against hope. Faith's logic is not couched in tentative expressions, such as *probably, perhaps, if, depending on,* but in courageous affirmations with all the force of *nevertheless or yes, but.* These are the affirmations that pit faith against despair and snatch victory from the jaws of defeat. This is the faith that becomes a source of vital new energy given by God, an energy at once supernatural and miraculous, that makes the impossible entirely possible. For a faith like this, waiting is not the falsification of hope but merely the duration between the promise and the fulfillment, between the "no longer" and the "not yet."

Thus the known facts may all be against God. But knowing God, we know that the known facts are not all the facts. So where we are going gives strength to what we are doing; and what we are doing is a sign of where we are going. Seeing God, we can wait, and trusting God, we can work on while we wait. This is the vision to which we are called.

> Nothing that is worth doing can be achieved in our lifetime; therefore we must be saved by hope. Nothing which is true or beautiful or good makes complete sense in any immediate context of history; therefore we must be saved by faith.
> —Reinhold Niebuhr

> And while it shall please thee to continue here in this world where much is to be done and little to be known, teach me by thy Holy Spirit to withdraw my mind from unprofitable and dangerous inquiries, from difficulties vainly curious, and doubts impossible to be solved. Let me rejoice in the right which thou hast implanted, let me serve thee with active zeal, and humble confidence, and wait with patient expectations for the time in which the soul which thou receivest, shall be satisfied with knowledge. Grant this, O Lord, for Jesus Christ's sake. Amen.
> —Samuel Johnson

Picture a small boy frustrated with a jigsaw puzzle because he is certain that the pieces do not fit the picture on the box. We are like this when we doubt. Each doubt makes us feel that this time we have found a real problem with God. But shake the pieces up a little, rearrange the one or two that we have put in the wrong place and everything changes. It is not the fault of the puzzle or the picture but the boy.

It is the same with our doubts. What we begin by calling God's problem ends up being seen as our problem that God solves. As the curtain falls on our discussion let this conclusion linger in our hearts and minds: The problem of doubt is not ultimately a matter of God's faithfulness but of our faith, just as the answer does not ultimately depend on our faith but on God's faithfulness.

This should make us prepared to take all our doubts to God straight away, though with the help of Christian friends. Doubts that are not resolved will inevitably blame God in the end. But is it right to allow each doubt to blame God in the beginning? Any unresolved doubt will tend to thrust us away from God, but our experience of his resolving our previous doubts should encourage us to come nearer. The first reaction of our hearts should echo William Cowper's prayer, "Decide this doubt for me."

If we are resolved to discard all inadequate grounds of trust, to abandon everything that will not hold us up, to reject all spurious foundations until our feet are on solid rock, then our faith will be single-minded and whole-hearted, a radical reliance on God that grips, and is gripped by, the faithfulness of God when all else fails.

We cannot guarantee that our faith will not fail, even when faith is single-minded. And when we are in two minds, we cannot enjoy God and we do not feel we can count on him. But God is more certain, more faithful, and more gracious than our doubting views of him. So the better we know ourselves, the more inappropriate we know it is to trust in our own promises or vows. When all is said and done, we are still ignorant, weak, and sinful. How much better it is to pray. Even the most devastating doubt remains faith and does not become unbelief when we pray. Each of us, however confident we are, may be a doubter, so this doubter's prayer should strike a chord in all our hearts:

> *Dear Lord,*
> *Although I am sure of my position,*
> *I am unable to sustain it without Thee.*
> *Help Thou me, or I am lost.*[1]
> —Martin Luther

NOTES

—■—

PART ONE:
I AM, THEREFORE I DOUBT

CHAPTER 1: I BELIEVE IN DOUBT

1. John 5:44.
2. Richard Sibbes, "The Bruised Reed and the Smoking Flax" in *Works of Richard Sibbes*, Vol. I, p. 85.

CHAPTER 2: DARE TO DOUBT

1. Eugene Nida, *God's Word in Man's Language* (Pasadena: Wm. Carey Library, 1973), pp. 123-24.
2. James 1:6.
3. Mark 11:23.
4. Luke 12:29—the only New Testament use of the word.
5. Luke 24:38.
6. Matthew 14:31.
7. Matthew 28:17.
8. For example, Luke 24:41.
9. Mark 9:24, RSV.
10. Martin Luther, *What Luther Says: An Anthology*, ed. Ewald M. Plass (St. Louis: Concordia, 1959), p. 1392.
11. See Romans 8:15-16, 23; 2 Corinthians 1:22; 2:21; Ephesians 1:14; 1 Thessalonians 1:5.
12. James Boswell, *The Life of Johnson* (Harmondsworth: Penguin, 1979), p. 227.
13. John Bunyan, *Pilgrim's Progress* (Harmondsworth, England: Penguin, 1965), p. 157.

PART TWO:
SEVEN FAMILIES OF DOUBT

CHAPTER 3: FORGETTING TO REMEMBER

1. Matthew 5:3.
2. Alexander Dru (ed.), *The Journals of Kierkegaard* (London: Fontana, 1958), p. 245.
3. 1 Corinthians 15:10.

4. Genesis 3:1, RSV.
5. Fyodor Dostoevsky, *Notes from Underground in Existentialism from Dostoevsky to Sartre*, ed. Walter Kaufmann (New York: Meridian Books, 1956), p. 74.
6. Romans 1:21.
7. Deuteronomy 5:15.
8. Deuteronomy 8:2.
9. Deuteronomy 6:11-12; see also Deuteronomy 4:9.
10. Exodus 13:3-9.
11. Numbers 15:38-39; see also Numbers 16:40.
12. Psalms 106:7,13.
13. Nehemiah 9:25-26.
14. Hosea 13:6.
15. 1 Corinthians 4:7.
16. Luke 7:47.
17. Luke 15:31.
18. See also Judges 2:7, 10; 3:7; Jeremiah 2:32; Ezekiel 15:7.
19. Augustine, *Confessions* (Harmondsworth, England: Penguin, 1961), p. 35.
20. Humphrey Carpenter, *W. H. Auden: A Biography* (London: Unwin Paperbacks, 1983), p. 449.
21. Grace Irvin, *Servant of Slaves* (London: Oliphants, 1961), p. 433. Titian's "An Allegory of Prudence" is in the National Gallery, London.
22. Luther, p. 1415.
23. Ibid., p. 1416.
24. John 14:26 and 16:8-10.
25. 1 Chronicles 16:34-35.
26. William Bradford, "Of Plymouth Plantation" in Perry Miller (ed.), *The American Puritans: Their Prose and Poetry* (New York: Doubleday Anchor, 1956), p. 18.
27. Saint Augustine, *Confessions*, Book 10 (Harmondsworth: Penguin, 1961), p. 231.
28. 1 Samuel 7:12.

CHAPTER 4: FAITH OUT OF FOCUS

1. Oswald Chambers, *My Utmost for His Highest* (New York: Dodd, Mead & Company, 1935), October 31.
2. Numbers 33:55.
3. 1 Kings 18:21.
4. Joshua 24:15.
5. C. S. Lewis, *A Grief Observed*, p. 76.
6. C. S. Lewis, *Letters to Malcolm: Chiefly on Prayer* (New York: Harcourt Brace & Company, 1963, 1992), pp. 81-82.
7. See Peter Brown, *Augustine of Hippo* (London: Faber & Faber, 1967), p. 345.

8. Pascal, p. 125.
9. Matthew 7:20.
10. Genesis 18:13-14.
11. Mark 1:40.
12. Mark 9:22.
13. Mark 1:41.
14. Mark 9:23.
15. Zechariah 8:6.

CHAPTER 5: NO REASON WHY NOT

1. Those who wish to pursue the question of verification itself may wish to consult such books as F. F. Bruce, *The New Testament Documents: Are They Reliable?*, (Downers Grove, Ill.: InterVarsity Press, 1960) and Michael Green, *Runaway World* (Downers Grove, Ill.: InterVarsity Press, 1968), both of which discuss many of the facts in question, or the present author's *The Dust of Death* (Crossway Books, 1994), Chapter 9, which discusses the idea and place of verification.
2. Quoted George Steiner, *Tolstoy or Dostoyevsky: An Essay in the Old Criticism* (New York: Vintage Books, 1957), p. 291.
3. Peter L. Berger, *The Precarious Vision* (New York: Doubleday, 1961), p. 158.
4. Peter Brown, *Augustine of Hippo* (London: Faber & Faber, 1967), p. 110.
5. 1 Peter 3:15.
6. Violet Bonham Carter, *Winston Churchill: An Intimate Portrait* (New York: Harcourt Brace, 1965), p. 19.
7. Ibid., p. 20.
8. Tolstoy, p. 464.
9. Genesis 15:6.
10. Genesis 15:8.
11. Genesis 15:13.
12. John 20:29.
13. John 4:53.
14. Acts 17:11-12.
15. John 20:30-31.
16. Luke 24:11.
17. Luke 24:12.
18. Acts 11:18.
19. Luke 17:21, AV.

CHAPTER 6: AN UNSIGNED CONTRACT

1. Robert Knille (ed.), *As I Was Saying: A Chesterton Reader* (Grand Rapids: Eerdmans, 1985), p. 265.

2. Vincent Donovan, *Christianity Rediscovered* (London: S.C.M., 1982), p. 62.
3. Ibid., p. 63.
4. G. K. Chesterton, *Orthodoxy* (London: John Lane, 1909), p. 55.
5. 1 Peter 1:22.
6. Pascal, p. 208.
7. Joshua 24:15.
8. Daniel 3:16-18.
9. 2 Timothy 1:12.
10. Henry Bettenson, ed., *Documents of the Christian Church* (London: Oxford University Press, 1963), p. 14.
11. Ibid., p. 283.
12. Ibid., p.4.
13. Alan Watts, *Beyond Theology* (New York: Meridian Books, 1969), p. 20.
14. C. S. Lewis, *A Grief Observed* (London: Faber & Faber, 1966), p. 32.
15. Revelation 14:12; see also 13:9-10.
16. Martin Luther quote—unknown source.

CHAPTER 7: NO SIGN OF LIFE

1. Georges Bernanos, *The Diary of a Country Priest* (London: Collins, 1956), p. 105.
2. Charles Darwin. *The Autobiography of Charles Darwin, 1869-1892* (London: Collins, 1958), pp. 86-87.
3. C. S. Lewis, *Mere Christianity* (London: Collins, 1955), p. 122.
4. C. S. Lewis, *The Letters of C. S. Lewis to Arthur Greeves* (NY: MacMillan Pub. Co., 1979) (24 December 1930), p. 398-399.
5. Revelation 3:1.
6. Luther, p. 489.
7. George Whitefleld. *Whitefield's Journals* (London: The Banner of Truth Trust, 1960), p. 136.
8. 2 Corinthians 13:5.
9. See 1 Corinthians 9:25-27; 1 Timothy 6:12; 2 Timothy 2:3-4.
10. Bunyan, p. 120.
11. Ibid., p. 115.
12. Matthew 7:18-27.
13. Mark 3:33-35.

CHAPTER 8: COUP D'ÉTAT FROM WITHIN

1. Walter Hooper (ed.), *The Business of Heaven: Daily Readings from C. S. Lewis* (London: Collins, 1984), pp. 76-77.
2. C. S. Lewis, *George Macdonald: An Anthology* (London: Geoffrey Blue, 1946), p. 133.

3. Thomas à Kempis, *The Imitation of Christ* (Garden City, NJ: Doubleday, 1955), pp. 121, 88.
4. Pascal, p. 39.
5. James Thurber in *I Believe* (London: Allen & Unwin, 1969), p. 137.
6. 1 Kings 19:4.
7. Lamentations 3:18.
8. Oswald Chambers, *My Utmost for His Highest*, February 17.
9. Roland H. Bainton, *Here I Stand: A Life of Martin Luther* (New York: Mentor Books, 1955), pp. 284-285.
10. Bunyan, p. 155.
11. *The Letters of Abelard and Heloise*, trans. Betty Radice (Harmondsworth: Penguin Books, 1974), p. 94.
12. Ibid.
13. Pascal, p. 36.
14. Ibid., p. 39.
15. C. S. Lewis, *Mere Christianity*, p. 123.
16. Oswald Chambers, *My Utmost for His Highest*, December 21.
17. Pascal, p. 311.
18. 1 Kings 19:5-6.
19. Matthew 6:11.
20. Mark 5:43.
21. Nehemiah 4:9.
22. Oswald Chambers, *My Utmost for His Highest*, May 20.
23. D. Martyn Lloyd-Jones, *Spiritual Depression: Its Causes and Cure* (London: Pickering & Inglis, 1965), p. 20.
24. Pascal, p. 274.
25. Luther, p. 514.
26. Ibid., p. 482.
27. Lloyd-Jones, p. 21. Also see Psalm 73:15.
28. 1 Corinthians 9:26-27.
29. 1 Thessalonians 4:4.

CHAPTER 9: SCARS FROM AN OLD WOUND

1. Luke 24:41, RSV.
2. Verse 34.
3. Exodus 20:2-3.
4. William Shakespeare, *Measure for Measure (I, iv, 77-79)* in *The Complete Works* (London: Odhams Press, 1953), p. 93.
5. Augustine, p. 116.
6. 1 John 1:7.

PART THREE:
TWO TORTURING QUESTIONS

CHAPTER 10: WHY, O LORD?

1. Franz Kafka, *The Castle*, trans. Willa & Edwin Muir (Harmondsworth, England: Penguin, 1957), p. 290.
2. Quoted in Antony Flew and Alasdair MacIntyre, eds., *New Essays in Philosophical Theology* (London: SCM Press, 1955), pp. 103-04.
3. Quoted Simone de Beauvoir, *The Marquis de Sade* (New York: Grove Press, 1953), p. 56.
4. Lamentations 2:5.
5. John 13:7.
6. Luther, p. 483.
7. Lewis, *A Grief Observed*, pp. 10-11.
8. Bunyan, p. 174.
9. John 8:12.
10. Oswald Chambers, *Not Knowing Whither* (London: Simpkin Marshall, 1934), p. 123.
11. Job 23:8-11.
12. Psalm 23:4.
13. Isaiah 50:10-11.
14. Lamentations 3:2.
15. Oswald Chambers, *My Utmost for His Highest*, February 14.
16. Augustine, p. 84.
17. Quoted Monica Furlong, *Contemplating Now* (London: Hodder and Stoughton, 1971), p. 68.
18. Job 1:22.
19. Job 19.
20. Job 9:35.
21. Job 19:25.
22. Job 40:8.
23. Simone Weil, *Waiting on God* (London: Routledge and Kegan Paul, 1951), p. 66.
24. Lamentations 3:16.
25. Lamentations 3:24.
26. Bunyan, p. 64.
27. Psalm 28:1.
28. Gerard Manley Hopkins, *Poems & Prose*, ed. W. H. Gardiner (London: Penguin, 1953), p. 62.
29. Jean Paul Sartre, *The Devil and the Good Lord*, trans. Kitty Black (New York: Vintage Books, 1960), pp. 140-41.
30. Fyodor Dostoyevsky, *The Brothers Karamazov*, p. 295.
31. Elie Wiesel, *Night* (New York: Avon Books, 1969), p. 44.

32. Matthew 27:46.
33. Lewis, *A Grief Observed*, p. 25.
34. Roland H. Bainton, *Here I Stand: A Life of Martin Luther*, p. 290.
35. John 20:17.
36. Matthew 6:9.
37. George Steiner, *Tolstoy or Dostoyevsky: An Essay in the Old Criticism* (New York: Vintage Books, 1957), p. 291.
38. Ibid, p. 292.
39. Arthur Koestler, "The Misunderstanding," in *The Call Girls* (London: Hutchinson, 1972), p. 10.
40. Lewis, *A Grief Observed*, p. 81.
41. Ibid., p. 33.
42. *The Letters of Abelard and Eloise*, trans. Betty Radice (Harmondsworth: Penguin Books, 1974), p. 84.
43. William Shakespeare, *Macbeth* (IV, iii, 208) in *The Complete Works*, p. 991.
44. Augustine, p. 202.
45. 1 Thessalonians 5:17.
46. Lamentations 3:37-38, 41.
47. Augustine, p. 232.
48. Luther, pp. 510-11.
49. Augustine, p. 76.
50. Notebook entry, quoted Konstantin Modulsky, *Dostoyevsky*, trans. Michael A. Minihan (Princeton: Princeton University Press, 1967), p. 650.
51. George Macdonald, *The Marquis' Secret*, p. 58.

CHAPTER 11: HOW LONG, O LORD?

1. Roland H. Bainton, *Here I Stand: A Life of Martin Luther*, p. 190.
2. Hebrews 11:1.
3. Oswald Chambers, *Not Knowing Whither*, p. 146.
4. Thomas Goodwin, "A Child of Light Walking in Darkness," in *Works* (Edinburgh: James Nichol, 1861), p. 330.
5. Romans 4:17.
6. Hebrews 11:14.
7. Dorothy L. Sayers, *Strong Poison* (London: New English Library, Times Mirror Books, 1970), p. 33.
8. Oswald Chambers, *My Utmost for His Highest*, July 29.
9. Psalm 49:10, 12.
10. Isaiah 26:19; see also Psalm 49:7-15 and Hebrews 11:19.
11. Jeremiah 32:24-25.
12. Hebrews 11:13, 16.
13. Hebrews 11:35-37.
14. Hebrews 12:2.

15. John 12:27-28.
16. Johann Wolfgang von Goethe, *Faust*, trans. Bayard Taylor (New York: Modern Library, 1950), p. 55.
17. Revelation 10:7.
18. Luther, p. 1390.
19. Pascal, p. 256.
20. Job 13:15, AV.
21. 2 Kings 6:33.
22. Isaiah 7:9.
23. Isaiah 30:15.
24. Isaiah 40:31.

POSTSCRIPT

1. Luther, p. 479.